Will You Be Mine?

Will You Be Mine?

Domestic Partnership
San Francisco City Hall
February 14, 1991

by
Diane Whitacre

with Foreword by
Harry Britt
San Francisco Board of Supervisors

Crooked Street Press *San Francisco, California*

First printed January 1993

10 9 8 7 6 5 4 3 2

Manufactured in the United States of America

Library of Congress Catalog Card Number: 92-97486
Will You Be Mine?
Domestic Partnership
San Francisco City Hall • February 14, 1991
by Diane Whitacre

ISBN 0-9635588-0-3

San Francisco, California

Contents

Foreword

From the very beginning, the movement to gain recognition of domestic partners has been a love story. The stigmas attached to homosexuality have produced many forms of discrimination. None are more painful than the isolation of denied love.

Lesbians and gay men have adopted survival strategies that pursue safety at the expense of freedom. Fear of parental disapproval and social ostracism encourage self-protection over self-expression. The result has been a paralyzing repression of natural feeling and crushing loneliness.

The need to choose between freedom and safety has shaped the politics of lesbian and gay America. Lesbians and gay men have been vulnerable to abuse from a culture where homosexuality is offensive. The Gay Rights Movement began with that awareness. Strategies designed to lessen the pain of discrimination have played down the realities of homophobia and become appeals for toleration. "I just happen to be gay" has been the plaintive slogan of the fearful victim of homophobia. It offers a homophobic culture no more than its liberal members can handle.

The Gay Liberation Movement developed in the 60s and 70s in the gay ghettos of urban America. It led to a different kind of politics. It produced a generation of activists unwilling to compromise their sense of who they were for an illusion of acceptance. In San Francisco, drag queens and street people, accustomed to experiments in personal freedom, rallied around the charismatic Harvey Milk. His name became associated with a style of politics which insisted that safety without freedom was no victory. It challenged America to see her queer children as they really were.

In 1979, I found myself in Harvey Milk's seat on the San Francisco Board of Supervisors. Very little time had passed before I was contacted by lesbians and gay men experiencing discrimination based on exclusion from the institution of marriage. Couples whose life-styles were identical to traditional marriage were treated as single because of their sexual orientation. Benefits for spouses earned from employment were denied to them. Attempts to gain employment benefits legally, like adoption of one partner by another, only put off dealing with the real problem.

The problem has been taken on by committed attorneys. They argue against the second-class status of lesbian and gay relationships. Most compelling has been the struggle of lesbian and gay couples to keep custody of their children.

It has always been clear to me that visibility of our relationships was central to our strategy. By hiding behind our legitimate claims to privacy, we have allowed straight society to avoid coming to terms with the realities of our lives. Domestic partners legislation is a big step in making lesbian and gay couples legally visible.

On May 22, 1989, the San Francisco Board of Supervisors unanimously passed a resolution. It invoked "the right of every person to form private relationships of mutual caring and economic interdependence without fear of prejudice."

It stated that, "San Francisco has a tradition of respect for the rights of all citizens...to form primary relationships, to share intimacy, and to care for one another...[and will] work aggressively to end discrimination against people whose relationships are not socially sanctioned, particularly lesbian and gay couples who are denied recognition given to other couples."

The resolution provided a mandate to examine all city policies and practices for bias against lesbian, gay, and other unmarried couples. It led to Proposition K, the Domestic Partnership Ordinance passed by the voters of San Francisco in November of 1990.

Domestic Partnership took effect on Valentine's Day of 1991. Now, lesbian and gay couples from all over the world can register their relationships with the City of San Francisco. Some couples register privately, with an attorney or notary. I am glad to see that many couples take the opportunity to share their love for one another publicly.

At the heart of the domestic partners legislation is the acknowledgment of the fundamental right to love and the fundamental wrongness of government to legitimize homophobic discrimination. It recognizes the domestic realities of lesbians and gay men excluded from marriage and enables them to publicly share their love. Straight couples can celebrate their union as they view it outside the traditional celebration of marriage. It seeks to recognize relationships purely as what they are without homophobic and sexist assumptions.

In our increasingly varied society, institutions which do not evolve to match new diversity diminish in importance. Domestic partners are creating a new and exciting institution.

It holds great promise for the future.

Registering a Domestic Partnership honors love and affection. These are the qualities that constitute real families. The couples depicted in the pages that follow are laying the foundations for a healthier, more loving society.

Supervisor Harry Britt

From the Author

For the past several years, I have photographed couples getting married in San Francisco's City Hall on Valentine's Day. My black and white photographs include people from all over the world.

February 14, 1991 was the first day that Domestic Partnership took effect in San Francisco. It was a city ordinance that simply allowed any two people over the age of eighteen to register their intimate, caring relationship and promise to be responsible for each other's basic food and shelter. It took ten years from its inception to its passage and officially validated relationships for couples that could not or did not choose to marry. It was legislation for the gay and straight community that had all the quiet rumblings of an earthquake for a social change that was beginning to happen all over the country.

On that morning I photographed couples that were getting married, then stayed for the Domestic Partnership celebration at 3:00 P.M. Photographs of the ceremony outside on the steps of City Hall and of the couples walking down the stairs inside the rotunda captured the joy, relief, humor, pride, and affection that the partners felt. Finally, there was public recognition for relationships that were as valid to them as any heterosexual marriage.

After pulling the prints I realized that I had photographed an historic event and wanted other people to see the pictures. Without signed releases, they could not be exhibited.

The subject of Domestic Partnership intrigued me. When heterosexual couples marry, it is the beginning of a family. Was it the same with Domestic Partners?

I obtained the public records of filings of the first day and began a random contact of forty-five couples. All but two couples readily consented to a thirty minute taped interview.

In almost every case, I was invited into a home with evidence and memorabilia of years spent together. The couples had been partnered an average of six years. They spoke frankly, candidly, sometimes humorously, and revealed some painful truths about their lives and their families. They expressed the same wants, hopes, and needs as any heterosexual married couple. They were not really complicated and would not be worthy of writing a book about except for the stereotyped image of gay and lesbian couples.

The book took shape as a history of how Domestic Partnership came to be with statistics, documents taken verbatim, interviews with the opposition that addressed the legal, financial, and moral issues, what the Domestic Partners had to say, and of course, the photographs.

My thanks to Richard Labonté for his encouragement, to Jim Hollenbeck for the title, and to Harry Britt for writing the foreword. A special thanks to the partners who consented to interviews. This book is as much about them as it is about the law. Their comments have been enlightening, sensitive, and perceptive. Each is one small part of this book, but when taken as a whole, they become a powerful voice.

For me, this is a book about family and is written as much for the straight community as it is for the gay community, and for single people as well as those who are partnered. Most important, it is a book for the young, for that is where the future lies, families begin, and discrimination can be ended.

It is my hope that this book will enlighten us all about our diversity as individuals and couples, and give a new perspective to just one of the many forms of family that exist in America.

Diane Whitacre

A History of Domestic Partnership

How it all began

When Richard Reich died on June 21, 1981, Larry Brinkin took two weeks off from his job at the Southern Pacific Railroad to grieve for his friend and lover of eleven years.

His union contract stated that employees were allowed a three day paid bereavement leave if a member of their immediate family died. When Larry returned to his job and asked for his three days pay, his boss called the legal department. They said no. The union contract definition of immediate family was spouse, mother, father, sister, brother, children, stepfather, stepmother, mother-in-law, and father-in-law. It did not include his relationship with Richard.

Two weeks before Richard died, a co-worker had been given a three day bereavement leave to go to the funeral of his step-mother. He had never met her.

Larry decided to ask the union to represent him in a grievance against the Southern Pacific Railroad because they had denied him bereavement leave. It was during this time that he noticed a tiny blurb in the *Bay Area Reporter*. It said that Harry Britt of the San Francisco Board of Supervisors had concerns about the lack of rights of lesbian and gay couples. Anyone interested in talking about this issue should come to a meeting at City Hall.

Larry went to the meeting where he met Matt Coles, an attorney in private practice. Afterward, they discussed Larry's grievance. Matt suggested the American Civil Liberties Union who took on Larry's lawsuit and used Matt Coles as the cooperating attorney.

The case received a lot of publicity and was the first in history to use the term "Domestic Partnership." Where did the term come from? The original motivators were Tom Brougham from Berkeley, Supervisor Harry Britt, his Administrative Aide Bill Kraus, and Matt Coles.

Tom had been talking publicly for a long time about how unfair it was that married people used the gym at the university and that his partner couldn't. He wanted to do something about it.

Tom, Bill, Harry, Matt, and Steve Neuberger from Local 2 of the Hotel and Restaurant Employees and Bartenders Union, held meetings to draw up an ordinance dealing with the rights of non-marital couples. Before 1980, the term non-marital defined couples by what they were not, instead of what they were. The group wanted to find a better name to define the relationship. At one of those meetings, someone suggested Domestic Partnership.

They decided to use it, though nobody liked it. It sounded like you were talking about a commercial venture or about people, who for thirty bucks, would come in and clean your house. It was first used officially in Larry's case and continued to appear in articles, political thought and discussion, and in the law.

Why it all began

The proponents of Domestic Partnership wanted to end discrimination against life-styles and relationships that didn't fit into the traditional definition of family. They also wanted benefits. Society was not ready to accept two people of the same sex living together as a family. A Domestic Partnership was not the traditional husband-wife-children family, but simply another form of family that existed in America.

Soaring divorce rates, remarriages, and adoptions had created many new forms of family. Common law marriages, foster families, single-parent families, and step families had become acceptable. Opposite sex couples living together were not sanctioned by the religious community, and society refused to accept the homosexual family.

Domestic Partnership had its roots in the Gay Movement. The history of the movement reflects the progression from criminal and discrimination issues to individual rights and benefits.

In the 50s, 60s, and 70s, the focus was on the decriminalization of private sex between consenting adults and stopping the harassment of gay men and gay bars.

Discrimination existed in employment. The witch hunts of the McCarthy Era rooted out gays and lesbians from government jobs. People weren't willing to be open about their homosexuality. There was blackmail. If you were openly gay, or arrested for a lewd conduct charge, you could be fired. Overt discrimination in employment and police harassment stemmed from gay men's sexual behavior. It was different from lesbians'.

The issue had little to do with lesbians, since men had most of the jobs and women didn't. Lesbians were suffering in silence on a case-by-case basis for visitation rights and child custody. Women realizing that they were gay got a divorce or found a lover. Their issues were mostly about children and challenging their fitness as a parent.

In the early 80s, the Gay Movement evolved into the Gay and Lesbian Movement. There were major successes in getting rid of some of the sodomy laws, police harassment, and abuse. The focus started shifting away from criminal and discrimination issues to individual rights. As people were discovering their identities and wanting to be open about themselves, gay rights became an issue. They wanted the right to get a job, to be promoted, and not to be fired. It had little to do with benefits. It was an individual rights movement for equal treatment and equal protection under the law.

Until then, relationship issues were in the background and benefit issues were almost non-existent. Then there was a shift to relationship and family issues beyond just children. Primary partners wanted to have their relationships recognized and wanted employment benefits. There were other people besides Larry Brinkin, who, with varying kinds of success, were going to court trying to get recognition from airlines, railroads, and other businesses.

In the mid-80s, the AIDS crisis took hold. Primary partners of gays and lesbians were going to hospitals. It was the blood relatives that had the right of visitation and medical decision-making. Partners that had been living together as a family did not have these rights. Wills and inheritances could be challenged. Without the AIDS crisis, these issues may not have emerged for decades. Domestic Partnership would give legal recognition to these relationships and help to provide the benefits.

What happened with State Legislation

In 1979, Jerry Brown, the Governor of California, issued an executive order prohibiting sexual orientation discrimination against any employee in the public sector who became openly gay or made an issue of his or her homosexuality.

Assemblyman Art Agnos introduced Assembly Bill 1 in the mid-70s. It made a very bold, across the board statement, that if you're gay or lesbian, you must be hired for a job if you're qualified. No one could fire or refuse to hire or not promote because of sexual orientation throughout the State of California. Agnos' predecessor, John Francis Foran, had been the first to introduce the bill to the Assembly. It was the Foran Bill or AB1386.

Every year, Art Agnos introduced AB1. It finally passed the legislature in 1984. Governor George Deukmejian vetoed it.

When Art Agnos left his post to run for Mayor of San Francisco, Assemblyman Terry Freidman introduced the same bill as AB101.

The Gay and Lesbian Movement wanted to get a clear cut statement by the legislature that such discrimination was prohibited, rather than patching together this court decision and this executive order and that local ordinance on the same subject.

Yet another Assembly Bill 101 went to the legislature in 1991. It did one thing; it added sexual orientation to employment protections in the Fair Employment and Housing Act. Proponents argued that sexual orientation discrimination is not prohibited by state law explicitly, and that the executive order did not protect anyone in the private sector, only state employees.

Governor Pete Wilson vetoed AB101 and insisted that "California should and does presently treat sexual orientation as a private matter, protected by the express right of privacy contained in the California Constitution, and entitled to legal protection in...specific areas [such as] housing and employment."

The gay community was outraged.

The First Domestic Partnership Ordinance

Matt Coles authored the first Domestic Partnership ordinance introduced in San Francisco by Supervisor Harry Britt in 1982. It passed the Board of Supervisors and was sent to Mayor Dianne Feinstein.

When it was first introduced, the language was like writing a blank check. It said that wherever married couples are granted benefits in the law in San Francisco, that Domestic Partners shall be granted the same benefits. The City's Budget Analyst predicted that it would cost the City nothing because the only significant benefit given to couples was health insurance to City Employees.

Harry Britt recalled, "She was clear with me that she liked the fairness part of it. She certainly wanted to be supportive of gay relationships. She didn't want to rock any boats, she didn't want to be a trail blazer, but she did want to do the right thing. She liked couples better than promiscuity. Certainly, there was pressure on her from the religious community and her Rabbi. I expected her to sign it. She appointed a task force that came up with a recommendation that you do it in a way to only include gay people. I could not support that because it would be a violation of our anti-discrimination ordinance."

Mayor Feinstein was lobbied heavily by the Catholic Church, the Archdiocese, and the Fundamentalist Church, both publicly and privately. The Archbishop was upset that the ordinance would recognize those relationships. For the first time in the history of the United States, virtually in Western History, you would have the State saying that lesbian and gay relationships are legitimate. It would affirm that couples do live together outside of marriage and deserve a measure of recognition and legitimacy.

The media called it the "live-in-lover ordinance" with "live-in-lover benefits." They trivialized it and didn't see its significance. Focus was on the sexual aspect of the relationships. It was pushed as a gay issue and not one for heterosexual couples.

Mayor Feinstein said that she was not going to sign a "blank check." She vetoed it. Her veto message said blood relatives had been excluded and there might be many who would want to be Domestic Partners to get health benefits. She did issue an edict that City Employees would be able to take bereavement leave if a member of their household died.

Matt Coles said, "From the very beginning, the core religious opposition understood the ordinance, in some ways, better than some of the supporters. This was not about health insurance, not about giving benefits, it was about getting society to see gay people and heterosexual couples differently. It was about showing the public there were couples with important intimate, supportive relationships that didn't define themselves through marriage. That was critically important to gay people. Part of society's idea is that gay people lead a cut off existence and are incapable of any kind of emotional depth. To get into the public's mind that these kinds of relationships were out there, would take a swipe at that stereotype."

Berkeley and West Hollywood

In 1984, Berkeley became the first city to pass a Domestic Partnership Employment Policy for City Employees. It specifically included opposite sex couples as well.

In 1985, West Hollywood passed Domestic Partnership with a "magic wand" approach to government. No studies, no task force, no research; they just voted and did it. West Hollywood had just incorporated and voted in a new City Council of five members, three of whom were openly gay. The Council's first act was to pass Domestic Partnership.

There were no real benefits attached; all it did was allow people to register their relationships. It allowed visitation in jails, but that was an illusory benefit. There were no jails, except one Sheriff's substation. People were held there for a day or two before they went to the County Jail. Hospital visitation wasn't a real problem. Domestic Partnership was symbolic and got coast-to-coast coverage.

The Second Domestic Partnership Ordinance

In May of 1989, Harry Britt introduced an updated Domestic Partnership ordinance written by Matt Coles. It included the registration system, making it different from any other in the country. There was bereavement leave, family sick leave, and the City could not discriminate against Domestic Partners. It created an official way of becoming partners without religious sanction. It passed unanimously and Mayor Art Agnos signed it.

On the day it was to become law, the opposition turned in enough signatures to put it on the ballot as a referendum. It was Proposition S.

"There were really only two issues on the ballot that year," said Harry Britt, "Prop S and the Ball Park Proposal. Art Agnos was more of a problem than Dianne. She didn't get involved in it and Art Agnos did. Art had a very irritating way of putting out press releases about how gay people were supporting the Ball Park and how the Giants were supporting Domestic Partnership. The Ball Park was unpopular with the left. The economics of Prop S, the way it was written, bothered the conservatives. They didn't really care one way or the other about the issue, but they voted in a low turnout election against the Ball Park. If the Ball Park issue had not been on the ballot and Art Agnos would not have been the mayor, we would have won it. The other reason Prop S failed was the City Controller, Sam Yockey. He put a statement in the voter pamphlet saying Prop S could produce a significant cost. This was not true. Conservatives always vote against anything that would increase costs. I was furious with the man."

Three weeks before the election, on October 17, 1989, there was a major earthquake affecting much of San Francisco. Campaign efforts stopped to help with the earthquake relief. Prop S lost by a slim margin.

Perhaps one of the reasons it failed, was that a lot of gays and lesbians didn't see it as their issue. Leaders were pushing the Domestic Partnership agenda and virtually ignoring the rights of single people to equal pay in the work place. Most adults in the gay community were not partnered, they were single. All the energy was going into giving Domestic Partners the same and equal treatment as those who were married.

There was the potential of liability to creditors of the two people who registered. Many questions were asked. Once you were responsible for "basic food and shelter," how long were you responsible for that? You could file a Notice of Termination, but did that end the financial obligation? There had been no court decisions. There was the question of benefits from public assistance. If you were living with someone and sharing expenses, would their income count as your income? Could your benefits be reduced or cut off?

Thomas Coleman, the Executive Director of the Family Diversity Project in Los Angeles says, "For people who have benefits or might need benefits, there's a means test. If you live together with somebody and share expenses, then their income is counted as your income. Their income is deemed available to you. There's a pooling arrangement. It's under the Social Security law, under MediCare law and SSI law...Rulings were asked for by the agencies and they said yes, that's true, we will. Heterosexuals have faced this all the time living with a person of the opposite sex or a relative and their income being counted."

Matt Coles says, "No, they would not. The law takes into account money and support you actually get. It does not care what your relationship is. If you are married, it acts as if you had access to your spouse's income, even if you don't have access...that relies on a marriage. I have never heard of a report of a Social Service Agency treating a Domestic Partnership as a marriage. In the Social Security Act, it uses the word 'marriage' and defines it as a valid marriage under State Law."

The San Francisco Bar Association sponsored a forum to advise lawyers how to warn their clients who were considering Domestic Partnership. Some skeptics warned, "See a lawyer...don't register...this could backfire...you might lose all of your benefits if you register."

Harry Britt reflected, "It was very valuable that we lost Prop S. Had we won, it would have down played the issue. The fact that the Right challenged us, said that this was important to them. It made our community more vested in the issue."

The Third Domestic Partnership Ordinance

The Domestic Partnership Ordinance was back on the ballot again in 1990 as Proposition K. It was also back in the press.

Harry Britt; *Bay Area Reporter* article, **Vote 1990:**
"This registry will be the first official acknowledgment of lesbian and gay relationships in this country. In the past, we have won the right to be free of discrimination in some cities and states. We were recognized through our inclusion in the Hate Crimes Statistics Act. Employees in some cities can gain benefits for their partners. But never before has any community in this country said to us, "You are a part of society and deserve the same respect due all people."

An opposition newsletter, *Mind Matters Review,* #6 October 7, 1990, featured an article, **Homosexual Newspaper Deceives Its Readers on Prop K,** (referring to the *Bay Area Reporter*):
"This is the same homosexual newspaper with sex ads advertising, 'Steamy back room action,' 'hot gay action,' 'instant action, deep satisfaction,' and on and on. During the week between the two bashings by *B.A.R.* against the flyers urging no on Prop K, Center for Disease Control announced that 75% of the homosexual population still take no precaution against the spread of AIDS by using condoms despite the devastation that AIDS is wreaking on the health care system...To be sure, we, meaning Coalition to Fight Fake Moralists, under the sponsorship of *Mind Matters Review,* intend to do everything in our power to drive homosexuality back into the closet where people who suffer from the psychological problems behind it will seek appropriate counseling."

The Examiner Herb Caen's column **Monday-Go-Round:**
ONWARD: The term "homophobic" is overworked and often misused, but it seems to me that a vote against Prop K (domestic partners) would be a form of gay bashing. Dean Alan Jones of Grace Cathedral says it best: "The proposed legislation is a small but significant contribution in building up the idea of the extended family again. Far from undermining heterosexual commitments, the proposed legislation reinforces them by insisting on the seriousness of our being responsible to and for one another."

The San Francisco Independent, June 19, 1990 article, **Mayor Floats New Domestic Partners Policy,** quotes David Gilmour, head of San Franciscans for Common Sense...
"When you start legitimizing these kinds of homosexual relationships, you're contributing to the moral breakdown of society."

Bay Area Reporter, October 30, 1990 article, **Open Forum - No on K** by Joseph P. Russoniello:

"Lets look at Prop K without the name-calling and the personal attacks and consider another point of view. I believe the proposition is more than a registration process for unmarried heterosexual and same-sex couples at City Hall. It is a financial time bomb, a legal nightmare and an anti-family measure that, if passed, will financially and socially impoverish San Francisco for years to come.

Though supporters of the current domestic partners ordinance say it will pay for itself through registration fees, the real financial impact will come after Prop K passes, when the activists and the politicians will do what they tried to do last year: endow live-in companions of all sexual orientations with health benefits, pensions and other monetary rewards that we, the taxpayers and consumers, will be forced to pay for.

...Domestic partners is more than just a financial time bomb. It is legal chaos just waiting to happen. If you can understand the pseudo-legalese of the proposition in your voter's handbook, you know that the domestic partners agree to share "basic living expenses." I pity the creditor who is owed money by one domestic partner who tries to collect his money from the other. The domestic partners ordinance is ambiguous, contradictory and full of vague generalities."

San Francisco Examiner, October 14, 1990, **Letters to the Editor:**

"It takes both courage and intelligence to speak out against the forces of hatred and social destruction represented by the religious groups who oppose passage of Proposition K, by those who wish to deny lesbians and gays positive interactions with children (even the children of lesbians and gays themselves), and by people like George Bush who say that no more money is needed to fight AIDS.

As a person who lives daily and painfully with the oppression so many straight people do not seem to even see, I am grateful to those who care."

R. Wood Massi, San Francisco

"I find your editorial, "Yes on domestic partners," very disturbing and in many respects unkind toward those people who are referred to as "narrow-minded with self-serving views on morality."

It is not true that we who reckon ourselves Christian manifest a "religion of hate." It is true that real Christianity is about love but it is not a compromising love with those that are considered evil and detrimental to the life of our communities.

In regard to "tolerance and understanding," we should not be expected to bombarded with the motto, "Say no to drugs." It is now high time that we include another motto, "Say no to homosexuality."

T. Fred Sandry, Belmont

"Thank you for backing Proposition K, the Domestic Partners legislation. The deep prejudices and negativity of the Roman Catholic and fundamentalist churches resounds clearly in the letters to the editor.

These good folk would rather put blame on non-married persons than face the fact that the Western World has undergone a sexual revolution. Clinging desperately to an outmoded view of family, these folk give religion a bad name. We clergy and lay people, sadly, get tarred with the same brush as these Neanderthals."

Rev. R. W. Cromey, Trinity Episcopal Church, San Francisco

A *Bay Area Reporter* article on October 11,1990:
Jean Harris, an aide to Harry Britt and coordinator of the Yes on Prop K campaign, said, "This is about lesbian and gay civil rights. We're not trying to pretend it's not. We're telling people who are in power that they can't define family anymore, they can't define our relationships anymore."

The following information was supplied to the voters:

City & County of San Francisco Consolidated General Election November 6, 1990

Proposition K
Shall two unmarried, unrelated people over the age of 18 who live together and agree to be jointly responsible for their basic living expenses be allowed to formally establish their relationship as a "domestic partnership?"
Analysis by Ballot Simplification Committee
The way it is now: There is no process for lesbians and gay men to formally establish and record their relationships.
The Proposal:
Proposition K would allow two unmarried, unrelated people over the age of 18 who live together and agree to be jointly responsible for their basic living expenses to formally establish their relationship as a "domestic partnership." They would establish their relationship by signing a Declaration of Partnership and either (a) filing the Declaration with the County Clerk or, (b) having the Declaration notarized and witnessed and given to the witness. A filing fee

would be charged to cover the City's costs.

The domestic partnership would end if one partner notifies the other that he or she has ended the partnership, if one of the partners dies, if one of the partners marries or if the partners no longer live together. When the domestic partnership ends, the partners would incur no further obligation to each other.

A person who has filed a Domestic Partnership Declaration may not file another such declaration until six months after the partnership has ended, unless the previous domestic partnership ended because one of the partners died.

Arguments for and against this measure

Proponent's argument in favor of Proposition K

Proposition K, the Domestic Partners registry, is simply a question of fairness. Proposition K will cost the city nothing.

Proposition K will allow lesbian, gay and other committed couples to register their relationships.

Under state law, lesbian and gay couples cannot get married. Despite their commitment, despite their love, despite all the joy and struggles they've endured, their relationships are neither recognized nor supported. Like all couples, they want visible recognition from their friends, families and neighbors.

This is an issue of choice and civil rights. Everyone has the right to choose whom they will love. The religious opponents of domestic partners, who want to enforce their view of what constitutes a loving, committed relationship on everyone else, would deny social recognition and support for gay and lesbian relationships. Let's stop the injustices by voting yes on Proposition K.

The previous proposal for domestic partners caused concern over potential costs to taxpayers. But the registry under Proposition K is financially self-supporting with fees covering all costs. Proposition K provides no city or employment benefits to domestic partners.

Proposition K is the respect and support that will allow all of the residents of our city to proudly say, "We are part of the family of San Francisco."

Submitted by the Board of Supervisors

Rebuttal to proponent's argument in favor of Proposition K

The Blitzkrieg-defying traditionalist Sir Winston Churchill–the man who destroyed Adolf Hitler–at age 13 memorized these fateful lines from Macaulay's Lays of Ancient Rome:

"Then out spake brave Horatius,
The Captain of the Gate;
To every man upon this earth
Death cometh soon or late.

And how can man die better
Than facing fearful odds,
For the ashes of his fathers,
And the temples of his gods?"

San Francisco's misguided Board of Supervisors purports to advise us on "Love," "Fairness" and so-called "Religion." Their ideas are flawed and twisted. Vote "NO" on Proposition K.

Even the claim that "domestic partners" will not cost us tax money is false. In light of the California case of Marvin v. Marvin (on the "implied contract' rights of "live-in" lovers), it's total folly to pretend that "domestic partners" will not open up the floodgates of future litigation. We can expect lots of court costs if Proposition K passes.

The First Amendment to the U.S. Constitution wisely bans the "establishment" of religion. The power of the state should not be used to advance particular creeds or belief systems.

Proposition K represents nothing but an attempt to "establish" the belief system of "domestic partners" as the official policy of the City and County of San Francisco.

The Board of Supervisors are insulting you and wasting your tax money by putting this already defeated "domestic partners" measure back on the ballot again.

Patrick C. Fitzgerald
Democratic Party Nominee for State Senator

Opponents' argument against Proposition K

JUST SAY "NO" TO "DOMESTIC PARTNERS"

San Francisco is a broad-minded seaport town.

People from all over the world have come to San Francisco since the day the Spanish navigator Ayala first sailed his ship through the Golden Gate.

The San Francisco Presidio's Lyon Street Gate and its ancient Officers Club are still guarded by the cannons of the Spanish King Carlos III.

The quartered arms of Aragon and Castile–the old banner of Imperial Spain–no longer flies over San Francisco.

San Francisco is a City with tradition.

San Francisco does not need the misguided Supervisor Harry Britt's proposed "domestic partners" law.

San Francisco and its voters defeated an almost identical "domestic partners" measure last year.

Still earlier, when Dianne Feinstein was still Mayor, the San Francisco Board of Supervisors passed another "domestic partners" resolution. Mayor Feinstein correctly vetoed that unwise proposal.

Now–like a Bad Penny–"domestic partners" has come back to again haunt the City and County of San Francisco. "Domestic partners" is basically a slap in the face to 3,000 years of Judeo-Christian-Islamic civilization:

That is the reason Archbishop Quinn last year had a letter read in every San Francisco Roman Catholic church attacking the 1989 "domestic partners" ballot measure.

That is the reason virtually every Catholic, Protestant, Eastern Orthodox, Jewish, Moslem, and Buddhist clergyman in the City and County of San Francisco agreed.

The truth is that "domestic partners" is a piece of legislation that would have been laughed out of the late Emperor Nero's pagan Roman Senate.

In fact, there is only one man in Suetonius' Lives of the Twelve Caesars who would probably have backed 'domestic partners' legislation.

His name???; The mad Emperor Gaius Caligula.

Gaius Caligula also put a horse in the Roman Senate.

Citizens Against "Domestic Partners"
Patrick C. Fitzgerald
Democratic Nominee for State Senator
Chairman of Citizens Against "Domestic Partners"

Rebuttal to opponents' argument against Proposition K

Domestic Partners is obviously NOT about Caligula. It is not about Imperial Spain, or King Carlos III, or about sailors crossing the Golden Gate.

It IS about our respect for one another. It's about the acceptance and recognition of our differences. It's about our willingness to tell our neighbors and families and friends that all people should be granted the right of being allowed to publicly recognize the one they love.

Yes, San Francisco is a city of traditions...Traditions of tolerance, fairness, and respect for others. Proposition K reaffirms these San Francisco traditions.

Please vote YES ON K.

Submitted by the Board of Supervisors

The Election

Between 1982 and 1989, changes had already occurred in areas where the City might use marriage as a factor in leave and visitation plans in jails and hospitals. Proponents dropped the statement about the City's non-discrimination against Domestic Partners. Some people thought it would open up a whole can of worms about City Health Benefits. Many voters thought the ordinance was about the City Health Plan. It never was. The Board of Supervisors couldn't pass policy for the City Health Plan, only the Health Service System Board could do that. They got those questions out of the voters' minds, and Proposition K passed.

It simply provided a registration system for any two people, heterosexual or homosexual, not blood related, not married and over the age of eighteen, who lived together and had an intimate, committed relationship of mutual caring, and agreed to be responsible for each other's basic living expenses during their Domestic Partnership. There were no other benefits.

It included a non-public registration. Some couples feared that people would use the public registry to harass couples who signed up. Couples would be allowed to take the forms, fill them out and have them notarized. They would not be a matter of public record. Couples that did not work or live in the City and County of San Francisco could register using the private system. With alternative registration, it would be impossible to know how many Domestic Partnerships there were.

February 14, 1991

Mayor Art Agnos intentionally certified the ordinance on January 14, 1991 so it would take effect thirty days later on Valentine's Day. On the first day 251 couples filed for Domestic Partnership: 149 couples were gay, 87 couples were lesbian, and 15 were opposite sex couples.

Matt Coles recalls, "I had a great foreboding about that day. I thought it would turn into a circus. I thought the promenade down the steps, when it was described to me, was a dreadful idea. When I watched the first couple come down that set of steps, it looked like the wedding day, the reception, and the prom all rolled into one. I saw every couple who came through that day. Most of the people I had never seen before while working on Domestic Partnership. That day showed you, that just like the opposition understood the law better than a lot of its backers did, that ordinary people understood the law a lot better than a lot of the politicians and technocrats who worked on it. It was saying, to all you folks who have been excluded from this institution for all these years, 'We realize you have lives.'"

The Health Service System Board passed Domestic Partnership benefits and added them to the City Health Plan in April of 1991. The package was sent to the Board of Supervisors. They approved the resolution. Mayor Art Agnos signed it on June 21, 1991. Larry Brinkin was there. He had worked ten years for Domestic Partnership benefits. It was the tenth anniversary of Richard Reich's death.

STATISTICS

251 Couples filed on Valentine's Day 1991

11%	28 filed only as one of you working in San Francisco
45%	83 filed only as living together in San Francisco
54%	133 filed as working and living in San Francisco
(244) Total	
59%	149 Gay couples
35%	87 Lesbian couples
6%	15 Opposite Sex couples
(251) Total	

1,085 Couples Filed in First Year

17%	175 filed as one of you working in San Francisco
26%	275 filed as living together in San Francisco
57%	616 filed as working and living in San Francisco
(1,066) Total	
57%	620 Gay couples
31%	335 Lesbian couples
12%	130 Opposite Sex couples
(1,085) Total	(Terminations as of 2/14/92...18, 1.65%)

59 Couples filed on Valentine's Day 1992

12%	7 filed only as one of you working in San Francisco
40%	23 filed only as living together in San Francisco
48%	28 filed as working and living in San Francisco
(58) Total	
68%	40 Gay couples
29%	17 Lesbian couples
3%	2 Opposite Sex couples
(59) Total	

City Employee Health Insurance

171 Employees Filed for City Health Insurance for their Domestic Partner in 1991.

Gay	59	(34%)
Lesbian	39	(22%)
Opposite Sex	77	(44%)

175 Total

One of the biggest objections from the opposition to Domestic Partnership, was that it would cost the taxpayers money for City Employee Health Insurance. They feared that gays with AIDS would cause premiums to increase dramatically. Their campaign gave voters the impression that City Employee Health Insurance was part of the Domestic Partnership ordinance. It wasn't.

In the first six months of Domestic Partnership, 91% of the total heterosexual filings occurred before June 15th, the cut off time for filing for City Health Insurance. 44% of the City Employees who took advantage of putting their Domestic Partner on City Health Insurance were heterosexual because more heterosexuals are employed by the City.

Randy Smith - Director of Health Services for City Employees

"The ordinance [covering City Health Insurance] is just a generic ordinance that we use every year. Provided in the plans [in 1991]...was this expanded eligibility to include Domestic Partners. The issue of eligibility is entirely up to the Health Service Board. Basically, the Board of Supervisors approves the rates of employee contribution and the plans that are going to be offered to City Employees for the next fiscal year.

For the most part, the City is paying for the employee's health insurance, and for the most part, the employees are paying for any dependent's health insurance.

City Employees pay into a trust fund. [Premium increases are paid for out of that fund.] It didn't cost the taxpayers anything. Outside actuaries were called in. They gave a pessimistic opinion, assuming that everything that can go wrong with their predictions, does."

The health service premium was increased based on the results of the Mayor's Task Force, that 2,000 couples filing Domestic Partnership would be using City Health Insurance.

It cost the City Employee Trust Fund a $2,000,000 premium increase. There would be no refund on the premium paid from the trust fund for the difference between the estimated 2,000 and the 175 Domestic Partners that actually used the plan. It was a risk. If 6,000 would have signed up, the insurance companies wouldn't have been paid any more money.

Ordinance No. 176-89

File No. 216-89-1

Domestic Partners

Amending Police Code to add Article 40 prohibiting discrimination against domestic partners by city and county; providing procedures to establish and to give notice of termination of domestic partnerships; and prohibiting discrimination in hospital visitation rights.

Be it ordained by the People of the City and County of San Francisco:

Section 1. The San Francisco Police Code is amended by adding Article 40, Sections 4001 to 4010, to read:

Note: All language is new; additions and substitutions have not been underlined.

SEC. 4001. DISCRIMINATION AGAINST DOMESTIC PARTNERS

The City and County shall not discriminate against Domestic Partners or Domestic Partnerships in any way. This includes (but is not limited to) using marital status as a factor in any decision, policy or practice unless it uses Domestic Partnership as a factor in the same way.

SEC. 4002. DOMESTIC PARTNERSHIPS; DEFINITIONS AND INFORMATIONAL MATERIAL

(a) Domestic Partnership Defined. Domestic Partners are two people who have chosen to share one another's lives in an intimate and committed relationship of mutual caring, who live together and have signed a Declaration of Domestic Partnership in which they have agreed to be jointly responsible for basic living expenses incurred during the Domestic Partnership, and have established their partnership under Section 4005 of the Article.

(b) Additional Qualifications to Become Domestic Partners. To be Domestic Partners, neither person may be married, the two may not be related to each other in a way which would bar marriage in California, and both must be 18 or older. Any different Domestic Partnership of which either was previously a member must have ended more than six months before the new Declaration of Domestic Partnership was signed (but this requirement does not apply if the earlier Domestic Partnership ended because of the death of one of its members).

(c) "Live Together" Defined. "Live together" means that two people share the same living quarters. It is not necessary that the right to possess the quarters be in both names. Two people may live together even if one or both have additional separate living quarters. Domestic Partners do not cease to live together if one leaves the shared living quarters but intends to return.

(d) "Basic Living Expenses" Defined. "Basic living expenses" means the cost of basic food, shelter and any other expenses of a Domestic Partner which are paid at least in part by a program or benefit for which the partner qualified because of the Domestic Partnership. The individuals need not contribute equally or jointly to the cost of these expenses as long as they agree that both are responsible for the cost.

(e) "Declaration of Domestic Partnership" Defined. A Declaration of Domestic Partnership is a form, provided by the County Clerk, in which two people agree to be jointly responsible for basic living expenses incurred during the Domestic Partnership and that all the other qualifications for Domestic Partners are met when the Declaration is signed. The form shall be contained in a booklet or packet with the informational materials described in paragraph (f). The form will require each partner to provide his or her primary residence address. The form must be signed under penalty of perjury. Unless it is filed with the City, the form must be witnesses and notarized. The City Attorney shall prepare appropriate forms.

(f) Informational Material. The San Francisco Human Rights Commission shall prepare informational material which will describe ways individuals in committed relationships may give their relationships the legal effect they would like them to have. The informational material shall state that the City is not providing legal advice and assumes no responsibility for the accuracy of the information provided.

SEC. 4003. ENDING DOMESTIC PARTNERSHIPS

(a) Termination. A Domestic Partnership ends when:

(1) the partners no longer meet one or more of the qualifications for Domestic Partnership; or

(2) one partner sends the other a written notice that he or she has ended the partnership; or

(3) one of the partners dies.

(b) Notice of Termination.

(1) To Domestic Partners. When a Domestic Partnership ends, the partners must execute a notice of termination naming the partners and stating that the partnership has ended (hereafter "Notice of Termination"). The Notice of Termination must be dated and signed under penalty of perjury by at least one of the partners. If the Declaration of Domestic Partnership for the partnership was filed with the County Clerk the Notice of Termination must be filed with the Clerk; in all other cases, the Notice of Termination must be notarized and a copy given to whomever witnessed the Declaration of Domestic Partnership.

(2) To Third Parties. A Domestic Partner who has given a copy of a

Declaration of Domestic Partnership to any third party in order to qualify for any benefit or right must, whenever the Domestic Partnership ends, give that third party a copy of the Notice of Termination. If that partner has died, the surviving partner must give the notice of termination to those third parties whom she or he knows were given a copy of the Declaration by the deceased partner in order to qualify for a benefit or right. The Notice must be sent within 60 days of the termination of the Domestic Partnership.

(3) Failure to Give Notice. Failure to give notice as required by this subsection will neither prevent nor delay termination of the Domestic Partnership. Anyone who suffers any loss as a result of failure to send either of these notices may sue the partner who has failed to send the required notice.

SEC. 4004. LEGAL EFFECT OF DECLARATION OF DOMESTIC PARTNERSHIP

(a) Rights and Duties Created. Neither this Article nor the filing of a Statement of Domestic Partnership shall create any legal rights or duties from one of the parties to the other other than the legal rights and duties specifically created by this Chapter or other ordinances or resolutions of the San Francisco Board of Supervisors which specifically refer to Domestic Partnership.

(b) Duration of Rights and Duties. Once a Domestic Partnership ends, the partners will incur no further obligations to each other under this Article.

SEC. 4005. ESTABLISHING EXISTENCE OF DOMESTIC PARTNERSHIP

(a) Domestic partners may establish the existence of their Domestic Partnership by either:

(1) Presenting an original Declaration of Domestic Partnership to the County Clerk, who will file it and give the partners a certificate showing that the Declaration was filed by the clerk: or

(2) Having a Declaration of Domestic Partnership notarized and giving a copy to the person who witnessed the signing. (See Section 4002 (e) of this Article.)

(b) The County Clerk shall only accept for filing Declarations of Domestic Partnership submitted by Domestic Partners who have a residence in San Francisco, or where one of the partners works in San Francisco.

(c) Amendments to the Declaration. A Partner may amend a Declaration of Domestic Partnership filed with the County Clerk at any time to show a change in his or her primary residence address.

(d) New Declarations of Domestic Partnership. No person who has created a Domestic Partnership may create another until six months after a Statement of Termination has been signed and either (i) filed with the County Clerk if the Declaration creating the partnership was filed or (ii) notarized; provided, however, that if the Domestic Partnership ended because one of the partners died, a new Declaration may be filed anytime after the Notice of Termination has been filed or notarized.

(e) Evidence of Domestic Partnership. Anyone who requires a person to provide evidence of the existence of a Domestic Partnership must accept (but may chose not to require) as complete proof a copy of a Declaration of Domestic Partnership.

SEC. 4006. RECORDS, COPIES, FILING FEES

(a) County Clerk's Records. The County Clerk shall keep a record of all Declarations of Domestic Partnership, Amendments to Declarations of Domestic Partnership and all Notices of Termination received by the Clerk. The records shall be maintained so that Amendments and Notices of Termination are filed with the Declaration of Domestic Partnership to which they pertain.

(b) Filing Fees. The County Clerk shall charge a fee of $35 for filing Declarations of Domestic Partnership and shall charge a fee of $7 for providing certified copies of Declarations, Amendments or Notices of Termination. There will be no charge for filing Amendments or Notices of Termination.

SEC. 4007. VISITATION IN HEALTH CARE FACILITIES

(a) Patient Designation. Where a health care facility restricts a patient's visitors, the health care facility shall allow every patient to name those individuals whom the patient wished to allow to visit, unless:

(1) no visitors are allowed; or

(2) the facility determines that the presence of particular visitor named by the patient would endanger the health or safety of a patient or patients, or would endanger the primary operations of the facility.

(b) Domestic Partners Who Do Not Make Designations. If a patient with whom visiting is restricted has not made the designation provided for in subsection (a), and if the patient has not indicated that she or he wishes no visitors, the facility must allow the patient's Domestic Partner, the children of the patient's Domestic Partner, or the Domestic Partner of the patient's parent or child to visit, unless:

(1) no visitors are allowed; or

(2) the facility determines that the presence of a particular visitor would endanger the health or safety of a patient or patients, or would endanger the primary operations of the facility.

(c) Health Care Facility Defined. A "Health Care Facility" is any clinic, health dispensary or health facility licensed under Division 2 of the California Health and Safety Code, any mental hospital, drug abuse clinic or detoxification center.

SEC. 4008. RETALIATION

No person who seeks the benefit of this Article shall be discriminated against in any way for seeking that benefit. No person who assists someone else in obtaining the benefit of this Article shall be discriminated against in any way for such assistance.

SEC. 4009. ENFORCEMENT

(a) Civil Service Commission and Human Rights Commission. This Article may be enforced by the Civil Service Commission insofar as the actions, decisions, policies and practices at issue pertain to employees of the City and County in their capacity as employees. In all other respects, this Article may be enforced by the San Francisco Human Rights Commission pursuant to Sections 12A.5 and 12A.9 of the Administrative Code.

(b) Civil Action. This Article may be enforced by a civil action. A complaint to the Human Rights Commission is not a prerequisite to enforcement in a civil action. The plaintiff in such an action shall be entitled to recover only compensatory damages and no punitive damages.

(c) Remedies. Any court that finds that this Article has been violated or will be violated may use all the powers which it has to remedy or prevent a violation.

(d) Statute of Limitations. Any action to enforce this Article must be commenced no later that two years after the claimed violation.

SEC. 4010. OTHER LAWS

Nothing in this ordinance shall be construed to interfere in or mandate theexercise of discretion regarding matters over which any board or commission of the City and County has exclusive charter authority; or to conflict with any rights or requirements established by charter, state or federal law, including, but not limited to, the rights and obligations attendant to marriage under state and federal laws. Nothing in this ordinance shall be deemed to alter or to require the alteration of eligibility requirements for social service, public health, and other entitlement programs provided or administered by the City and County. Nothing in this ordinance shall be deemed to alter any existing memorandum of understanding to which the City and County is a party.

APPROVED AS TO FORM:

LOUISE H. RENNE
City Attorney   By:_____
                       Deputy City Attorney
                       (As amended at Board meeting of 5/22/89)
                       Board of Supervisors, San Francisco

Passed for Second Reading May 22, 1989
Ayes: Supervisors Alioto Britt Gonzales Hallinan Hsieh Kennedy Maher Nelder
Walker Ward
Absent: Supervisor Hongisto

Finally Passed May 30, 1989
Ayes: Supervisors Alioto Britt Gonzales Hallinan Hongisto Hsieh Kennedy
Nelder Ward
Absent: Supervisors Maher Walker

**I hereby certify that the foregoing ordinance was finally passed by the
Board of Supervisors of the City and County of San Francisco.**

_____Acting Clerk

_____Mayor

 JUNE 5, 1989
Date Approved
File No. 216-89-1

Domestic Partnership Information Sheet

prepared by the American Civil Liberties Union of Northern California.
Note: This isn't legal advice; only a lawyer can give you that.
Take a moment to read this before you sign.

This may not do all the things you want...

A domestic partnership isn't the same as a marriage. For instance,
unless you have a will, your partner won't get your property if you die. A
domestic partnership won't make sure that your partner has the legal
right to take care of you if you get sick. It doesn't mean that your partner
and you have a right to each other's pay or property. There are other
things you may want to do to protect your relationship.

Other things to do...

A Will

To make sure your partner gets your property when you die, you
need a WILL or another estate planning tool done by a lawyer. There
are do-it-yourself books on wills. It is safer to get legal advice, but using
a good do-it-yourself book is better than trying to do a will on your own,
and much better than delaying.

A Medical Power of Attorney

The only way to be sure that your partner can be in charge of your
care if you get sick is for you to do a DURABLE POWER OF
ATTORNEY FOR HEALTH CARE. These are easy to fill out. The San
Francisco Medical Society has free forms for this, and many lawyers do
them also.

Property and Pay

If you and your partner buy anything together, state law on property
owned by two people will cover it. A domestic partnership has no effect
on property ownership. It does not, for example, give you any right to
property which your partner pays for. A domestic partnership does not
give you or your partner any rights to each others' pay. Relationship
contracts can do these things. If you want to know more about your
rights, get legal advice.

Benefits

This law sets up a system which companies, stores, other
businesses, and unions may use to include domestic partners in family
discounts, leave policies, health plans, etc. But it doesn't make anyone
give any benefits to domestic partnerships. If you want your employer or
another business to accept domestic partnerships, you'll have to get
them to agree to do it.

This may do things you hadn't counted on...

A domestic partnership creates legal rights and duties. For example, you have to make sure that your partner has food and a place to live if she or he can't get those things.

You have commitments...

Basic responsibilities

If you sign a domestic partnership, you promise to make sure that your partner has basic food and shelter. This means that if he or she doesn't have food or can't afford his or her part of the cost of the place where you live, you must pay for these things.

It's a legal duty

If your partner can't get food or shelter for herself, she or he can make you get them. She or he could get a court order. If someone else gives your partner food for credit, for example, they can get you to pay. The same goes for your partner's part of the cost of the place where you live.

Sometimes, there may be more duties

Suppose you have health insurance from your job. If you convince your employer to cover your partner, you will be responsible for any medical bills the insurance doesn't pay (like deductibles or co-payments). This means that if your partner doesn't pay them, you have to, and the doctor or hospital can make you. The law is not intended to make domestic partners responsible for extraordinary food and housing costs (like room and board in a medical facility). But some lawyers fear that a court could decide that it does. Especially if you think one of you might get sick, you may want to get specific legal advice.

Other things to think about...

If you file your declaration with the County Clerk, it will be a public record. Anyone can look at it.

A public record

There are two ways to set up a domestic partnership. One way is to use the county clerk. If you do this, there will be a public record of your partnership. Anyone can see it. You can avoid this by using a notary.

Be careful with Welfare and Public Assistance

Domestic Partnerships won't affect State Disability Income (SDI) or Social Security Disability Insurance (SSDI). The Department of Social Services (DSS) says Domestic Partnerships won't affect benefits under the programs it runs. These include Medi-Cal, AFDC and GA. It shouldn't affect SSI. But some lawyers worry that it might affect both DSS programs and SSI. If either you or your partner gets public assistance (or if you might in the future) you may want to find out before you sign how a domestic partnership might affect these and other programs.

You've got to do it right...
It's easy to start a domestic partnership, but you need to do it right.

How to do it...

There are two ways
If you live in San Francisco, or if you work here, you can set up a domestic partnership with the County Clerk. Anyone can set up a domestic partnership using a Notary Public.

County Clerk
To set up a domestic partnership with the county clerk, you and your partner must both sign the form (the "Declaration of Domestic Partnership"). Both of you must then bring the form to the clerk's office. After you pay $35, the clerk will file the form and give you a Domestic Partnership Certificate.

Using a Notary
To set up a partnership with a notary public, you and your partner must take the form (the "Declaration of Domestic Partnership") to a Notary Public. You must go together. Both of you must sign the form in front of the notary. You must then give a copy of the signed form to a witness. The witness can be the notary or it can be someone else you pick.

Ending a partnership
A Domestic Partnership ends when: (1) one of the partners dies: (2) one of the partners sends the other a Notice For Ending A Domestic Partnership; (3) one of the partners gets married; or (4) the partners stop living together. The county clerk has instructions on how to end a domestic partnership.

YOU MUST READ THIS BEFORE YOU SIGN
To be domestic partners, you and your partner must live together (see below for an explanation of what this means), be 18 or over, and you must agree to be responsible for each other's basic living expenses. Neither of you can be married to anyone and neither of you can have a different domestic partner. If either of you had a different domestic partner before, you have to wait six months after the old domestic partnership ended before you can set up a new one. You don't have to wait if your old partnership ended because your partner died. You can't be related to your partner as a parent, as a child, a sister or a brother, an

aunt, an uncle, a niece, a nephew, a grandparent or a grandchild.

"Live Together"

"Live together" means that the two of you share a place to live. You don't both have to be on the rental agreement or deed. It is okay if one or both of you has a separate place somewhere else. Even if one of you leaves the place you share, you still live together as long as the one who left intends to return.

"Basic Living Expenses"

"Basic living expenses" means the cost of basic food and shelter. It also includes any other expense which is paid by a benefit you or your partner gets because of the partnership. For example, if you get health insurance from your job, and the insurance covers your partner, you will be responsible for medical bills which the insurance does not pay. You don't have to split basic living expenses to be domestic partners. You just have to agree to provide these things for your partner if he or she can't provide for him or herself.

SAN FRANCISCO

DECLARATION OF

DOMESTIC PARTNERSHIP

We declare under penalty of perjury:

1. We have an intimate, committed relationship of mutual caring;

2. We live together (see definition on the other side of this page);

3. We agree to be responsible for each other's basic living expenses (see definition on the other side of this page) during our domestic partnership; we also agree that anyone who is owed these expenses can collect from either of us;

4. We are both 18 or older;

5. Neither of us is married;

6. Neither of us is related to the other as a parent, brother or sister, half brother or sister, niece, nephew, aunt, uncle, grandparent or grandchild;

7. Neither of us has a different domestic partner now;

8. Neither of us has had a different domestic partner in the last six months (this last condition does not apply if you had a partner who died; if you did, cross this out).

We declare under penalty of perjury under the laws of the State of California that the statements above are true and correct.

Signed on _____, 19___ in _____

Signature _____ Print Name _____

Signed on _____, 19___ in _____

Signature _____ Print Name _____

YOU MUST ALSO FILL OUT THE OTHER SIDE OF THIS FORM

DECLARATION OF DOMESTIC PARTNERSHIP

1. Definitions:

"**Live together**" means that the two of you share a place to live. You don't both have to be on the rental agreement or deed. It is okay if one or both of you has a separate place somewhere else. Even if one of you leaves the place you share, you still live together as long as the one who left intends to return.

"**Basic living expenses**" means the cost of basic food and shelter. It also includes any other expense which is paid by a benefit you or your partner gets because of the partnership. For example, if you get health insurance from your job, and the insurance covers your partner, you will be responsible for medical bills which the insurance does not pay. You don't have to split basic living expenses to be domestic partners. You just have to agree to provide these things for your partner if he or she can't provide for him or herself.

2. Address: Each of you should fill in your mailing address here:

Name _____

Address _____

City, State & Zip Code _____

Name _____

Address _____

City, State & Zip Code _____

3. The Last Step: To finish setting up a domestic partnership, you must EITHER:

(1) File this form with the San Francisco County Clerk; or
(2) Sign this form in front of a Notary Public and have the Notary fill in the notarization at the bottom of this page.

To be able to file this form with the County Clerk, one of you must work in San Francisco OR both of you live together in San Francisco (see explanation below).

[ ] Check here to state that one of you works in San Francisco.
[ ] Check here to state that you live together in San Francisco.

You don't have to check either space if you finish setting up your domestic partnership by getting this Declaration notarized.

4. Notarization: Use only if you do not file the Declaration with the county clerk

State of _____

County of _____ ss.

On this _____ day of _____ in the year 19 ___ , before me _____ personally

appeared _____ , personally known to me (or proved

to me on the basis of satisfactory evidence) to be the persons whose names are subscribed to this instrument, and acknowledged that they executed it.

_____
Notary Public

DECLARATION OF DOMESTIC PARTNERSHIP

1991

DOMESTIC PARTNERS

CITY AND COUNTY OF SAN FRANCISCO

_____ , _____, CLERK OF THE CITY AND COUNTY OF SAN FRANCISCO, CERTIFIES THAT

_____ *and* _____

BECAME DOMESTIC PARTNERS BY FILING A DECLARATION OF DOMESTIC PARTNERSHIP IN THE OFFICE OF THE CLERK.

_____
COUNTY CLERK

BY _____
DEPUTY COUNTY CLERK

FAMILY REGISTRATION

Domestic Partnership does not define a couple as a family, but merely as partners. They are denied discounts, memberships, privileges and legal rights that recognized family members would have, even though they have accepted the emotional, financial, and community responsibilities of a family unit.

Thomas Coleman, Executive Director of The Family Diversity Project in Los Angeles, said, "I'm going to find a way for a state-wide [family] registry under existing law, so we don't have to get the legislature or the Governor to do anything."

He and his partner applied for a certificate from the Secretary of State, registering as an unincorporated, non-profit association.

Thomas concluded, "A family is that. A family is not a business, it is not a corporation, a family is an association because an association is a group of people with a common purpose or purposes. Therefore, a family is a type of unincorporated, non-profit association."

They registered as "The Family of Thomas F. Coleman and Michael A. Vasquez." At the time, they didn't think the State realized what they were doing. Thomas tried it again with a lesbian couple and it worked. He registered two step families, an unmarried couple, a guardianship family, a single parent guardianship family, and a foster family with disabled adult foster children. They represented family diversity and the geographic diversity of the state.

Then, rejection letters started coming back saying that a family is not an association that can register. Thomas had gotten beyond the clerk-typist level of scrutiny. He contacted the Secretary of State's office and talked to the Chief Deputy. He sent a legal memo as to why this was appropriate. March Fong Eu, the Secretary of State, said that it could be done.

Thomas did a computer search of state statutes that used the term "family." The computer found 1600 statutes. 167 used the term in a significant way...terrorist threats against immediate family members, extortion by threats to accuse a family member of a crime, phone calls threatening to injure your family member, victims' rights to have a family member at a court hearing, domestic violence diversion program, child abuse diversion program, the right to restitution from a convicted defendant, bereavement leave for school district workers that take time off if their immediate family member died, objecting to a referee if a referee is related to a family member of one of the parties, a refund in the bar exam fee if there's a death or illness in the immediate family, a nursing license is not required if you are family...those were just a few.

Family is built into many codes. In 75% of those 167, the term "family" was not defined. There is no one definition of "family" in American law or in California law. There is flexibility. The definition will depend upon the context in which it is used. If it is not defined, the judge or the administrator has to make the decision. They look to three criteria. Do the people consider themselves a family? How are they projecting themselves as a family to society? Do they function as a family unit? Family registration would satisfy the first two criteria.

Matt Coles, ACLU attorney in San Francisco, had another view, "People have to be careful with that...People have to remember it [the State Registry for an unincorporated, non-profit association] was not set up with intimate or family relationships in mind. It was set up for social relationships and social clubs and little charities that didn't incorporate themselves. When the 'family' comes to split up, the law that's going to get applied to that...is not California family law, it's the California non-profit association law and that might lead to some very bizarre results. They have to follow the law on dissolving unincorporated associations. You either have to get everyone in the association to agree to that or you have to petition the Superior Court to dissolve it. I don't know if the people who sign up for it exactly understand what they're getting into."

The Western Center for Law and Religious Freedom in Sacramento demanded that the Secretary of State stop registering "families" and un-register the ones that she did. There are about two hundred "families" that have registered with the State. About 85% of them are gay and lesbian relationships.

Thomas Coleman feels this will end up in court, and says, "Whether we win or lose, we're raising consciousness about the need for a mechanism for people to declare themselves. If society considers something important enough, they create a mechanism for authentication. Business partners can file a partnership – they can file a fictitious name statement, a corporation can file incorporation papers, if there's a birth – there's a birth certificate, if there's a death – there's a death certificate, if there's a marriage – there's a marriage certificate, if there's a divorce – there's a divorce decree, if there's an adoption – there's an adoption decree, if there's a change of name – there's a change of name decree. If it's important enough to society, there's a mechanism to authenticate it. That's why Domestic Partnership has come up, because there's a need for it."

The
Photographs

*taken at San Francisco City Hall
Valentine's Day 1991
and on the First Anniversary
of Domestic Partnership in 1992*

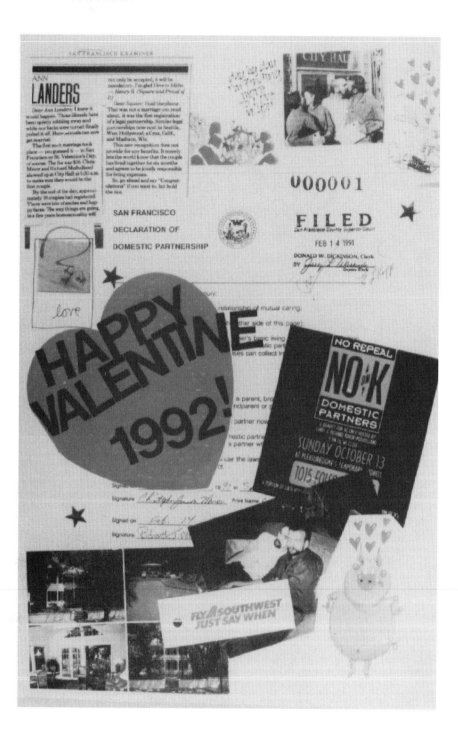

What the Opposition to Domestic Partners had to say...

The following are excerpts from taped interviews
with three opponents of Domestic Partnership
and a transcript of parts of a video tape
produced by a candidate
running for the Board of Supervisors.

Patrick C. Fitzgerald, 56, was the Democratic Party Nominee for State Senator in November of 1990 and the Chairman of "Citizens Against Domestic Partners."

Q   What started the whole idea of Domestic Partnership?
Mr. Fitzgerald: *The Board of Supervisors. Harry Britt had an idea. They wanted to have some kind of recognition for gays and lesbians. He had the idea that if they could get gays and lesbians and people of the opposite sex that were living together out of wedlock, some of them might want to go down to City Hall and have some sort of certificate for living together.*
Q   Why the need for it?
Mr. Fitzgerald: *There's a certain thing called friendship. You don't have to go down to City Hall and get a certificate to be somebody's close friend. I feel, that in a marriage relationship, you have legal responsibilities and you have kids and benefits that accrue from that, because you have minors that are not able to fend for themselves or take care of themselves. I think in adult relationships, if two people are living together, they should both be able to provide their own medical benefits. One shouldn't take the medical benefits because of living with the other. I don't see the dependency factor there.*
Q   Basically, it was a registration and the commitment to supply basic food and shelter to the other party.
Mr. Fitzgerald: *It opened the door. Supervisor Harry Britt...they were all saying that they weren't going to go for benefits. The first thing they did, after they got the Domestic Partners passed, is go for health benefits for City Employees. This thing could ultimately cost the taxpayers millions of dollars.*

They can try to pretend that there is no AIDS epidemic, but there is. When you get this particular group, you're getting into a high risk group that a lot of insurers might say, "Hey, you're high risk, we don't want to take you," but in the City Health Plan, they have to take them.

Some of these terminal things could end up costing with hospitalization. I don't see how the premiums are going to cover it. I don't think it makes good common sense to put in a high risk group. If I were sitting on the board of directors of an insurance company, I wouldn't want to write a high risk group because I'd know I'd have a lot of payouts. That could ultimately raise everybody's cost in the health plan.
Q   Why are you opposed to Domestic Partnership?
Mr. Fitzgerald: *They're pushing relationships, which an awful lot of*

the population would deem to be questionable; same sex relationships and so forth. A lot of people think that two gay men engaging in, what a lot of people would consider kinky sex or two lesbians engaging in kinky sex, is kind of a questionable relationship. I think it's probably got as much credibility as somebody going down to City Hall and wanting to get a certificate for getting drunk. That's a questionable activity, too.

I'm not anti-lesbian or anti-gay, as such, but I just think they lack a sense of propriety, what's right, and they want to push their agenda over community standards. They would like to stifle community standards, bury them, and pretend that they don't exist. For me, community standards are very real and they do exist. We resent these people trying to shove something like this down our throats.

Q   Domestic Partnership is optional. It's a choice that's there for them, if they have that type of relationship, to register that relationship and say we care enough about each other that we'll provide basic food and shelter for each other.

Mr. Fitzgerald: *As long as you keep the sex element out of it, but unfortunately, it's not out of it, it's right there.*

Q   Many heterosexual couples filed.

Mr. Fitzgerald: *They're not taking legal responsibility for things and what not. I think it's kind of a flaky way. I've been married for twenty-six years, and I think that's a flaky way to have a relationship. If you're going to have a relationship, go down and get married and do it the conventional way. I think that this is kind of a borderline type of thing.*

The Domestic Partnership never could have passed if the gays and lesbians didn't pull these other people in with them. There is such a thing as morality and a lot of us believe in it and we believe that a lot of the laws that are on the books are based on the moral law. A lot of these things people are doing, have been considered for a long time, to be immoral. I just can't see, at our San Francisco City Hall, going down and giving a certificate of merit to people for acts that a lot of people don't consider right or don't consider moral.

Q   How would you like to see the law or would you like to see any law that includes that segment of the population?

Mr. Fitzgerald: *They can still have friendship without going down to City Hall and getting a certificate of merit for it.*

Q   What do you think will happen in the future as relates to the Domestic Partners law?

Mr. Fitzgerald: *I don't think it's necessarily here to stay. I think it's probably going to be opposed again. I don't know if anything else if going to come from it. I think the fact that it's in, is unsatisfactory to me and a* *lot of other people. If we can get it out in the future, we're going to make an effort and try to get the thing out again.*

Q   Is there any other thing that's detrimental about it?

Mr. Fitzgerald: *It flies in the face of traditional family values. A lot of people in San Francisco adhere to traditional family values. I don't think they like the other side of town trying to say there's no such thing and sweep the whole thing under the rug and then feel, because they control City Hall, they can do anything they want to do.*

Q   Define traditional family values.

Mr. Fitzgerald: *The mother and father married, with or without children. The traditional monogamous relationship between a man and woman.*

Q   Would there have been as much opposition to Domestic Partnership if it would have applied to opposite sex couples only?

Mr. Fitzgerald: *I don't see what the point would be. They wouldn't have legal right of inheritance. If you're going to do something, you do it right or you don't do it at all. If they want to have a relationship, they ought to have enough guts to go down and get married. A lot of the religious groups certainly would have opposed it. There's a slang expression for that kind of thing. It's been going around since I was a kid. It's called shacking up and it wasn't particularly approved of.*

Q   What kind of couples do you think registered to be Domestic Partners?

Mr. Fitzgerald: *Probably a lot of people that feel that they're on the fringe of society and they probably wouldn't have what you consider a normal relationship. I'm sure a lot of them would be people that I would personally like. I'm against the concept. I'm not down on the group of people as such, I'm down on the thing that they are doing. I think we have to have voices in the community speaking out against it.*

Q   The statistics show that only a small percentage of the gay community took advantage of Domestic Partnership.

Mr. Fitzgerald: *Of course. The thing's in its infancy. It's just getting going. Maybe a lot of these relationships that the gay and lesbian leadership is touting so strongly, are not all that strong.*

END

George Wesolek, 47, is the Executive Director of the Justice and Peace Commission of the Archdiocese of San Francisco. He works on public policy issues. On the issue of Domestic Partnership, he is the spokesperson for the Archdiocese.

Q   Why was there a need for Domestic Partnership?
Mr. Wesolek: *My guess would be, and what they've stated, is that some felt that there was a need for a legitimation, publicly and civilly, of a reality of relationships that had already happened. It was really more of a symbolic thing in some ways. I think for some couples it probably had more real implications.*

The ordinance itself is a very vague kind of thing. It really doesn't outline any kinds of duties or responsibilities that you would normally have outlined in statutory law about a relationship like you do in marriage. That was one of our principal objections to it. It was so vague.
Q   Domestic Partnership was no more than just a registry.
Mr. Wesolek: *It was a very symbolic thing. In San Francisco, it takes on an added significance. It doesn't mean much in some ways, but certainly symbolically, to a whole group of people, it means a lot.*
Q   Why the opposition?
Mr. Wesolek: *I think it was on the symbolic grounds. That was really the issue. It was a real clash of values between those who would want to legitimize a non-traditional life-style and those who felt there was a need, in a public arena specifically, to protect and support traditional family arrangement and style. It reflected itself in the ordinance. That battle, that cultural clash, is going on still in a variety of different ways with similar kinds of ordinances in other parts of the country that do the same kind of thing.*

The way we look at it, speaking from the Roman Catholic tradition, is very clearly that marriage is for us, a sacrament. It isn't just a relationship, but it's something that two people commit themselves to until death, in Christ. There's a very strong theological, religious significance to marriage. In order to make that happen, you have to have two people that are willing to commit themselves forever to each other and then also have the intention of having children. The children are an integral part of that. Our position is pretty clear. That's what we hold and that's what we try to teach and that's what we ask our people to live. Everybody doesn't live that. There are a lot of divorces.

Then, you get into the whole area of public policy and what public law is supposed to do. Basically, from our point-of-view, it is to protect, what

we call the common good. A very central part of the common good is families. We feel families have been absolutely devastated.
Q   What has caused that devastation?
Mr. Wesolek: *I think it's a series of things. It's very strongly cultural, it's the "sexual revolution", it's our inability to commit permanently to someone. People from all walks of life deal constantly with the issue of commitment. How do we make something real, something solid, something that's going to last? In our day and age and the atmosphere that we live in, commitment's in trouble. It's a vicious cycle. A lot of people have come from broken homes. They're afraid of commitment because they saw some painful episode in their own lives, so they're very cautious. So, relationships become serial or fleeting or whatever.*

Not just from the moral standpoint is there a problem there, but just in terms of the good of society. What are we doing to the structure of our society for the future, not now? What really does society rest on? A lot of folks say, it rests on the stability of the family, that's the core unit at the bottom of it all. There is where you get a real cultural values clash when you talk about an issue like Domestic Partnership. Those concepts are very difficult to express in a political campaign. We feel that public policy should protect that family unit and not put out this law, even though some of the proponents said this would help committed relationships.

If you read the Domestic Partnership law very carefully, it is set up to help very impermanent relationships. There is nothing in the law that really binds people together. In marriage law, you have responsibilities. If I leave my wife, I'm not just going to leave her, but I am going to have responsibilities for her and for my children. None of that is in Domestic Partnership. It's like...gee, we happen to like each other and maybe there's a commitment and maybe there isn't. It's really open to abuse since none of that material is there to bind the couple together.

I think I would be the first person, if I had a friend who was dying of AIDS and they had no medical care, to get my $35 and sign them right up, because they don't have to live with me, they don't have to live in the same town.
Q   If the law would have been written for only heterosexuals do you think there would have been as great an opposition?
Mr. Wesolek: *Sure. It's like it's setting up an alternate track for marriage. So, if you are a parent and you're teaching your children about what marriage and what sex is all about and permanent commitment and very important values, and want them to share those values; if publicly, they look around and they see there's marriage, that's a lifelong commitment, 'til death do us part, and then there's this other thing that*

says we can sort of sign up if we want and it's real loose and it's only $35 and in six months I can write a letter and dissolve the thing anytime I want; I think that's a real poor message to be sending to kids in terms of education. That's a public kind of statement about what they're thinking of relationships. It's like your second track marriage. I'm talking mainly on the heterosexual part now. That's not what I want them to hear.

I realize that those kinds of relationships are going on all over the place, but I don't think public law should support that. Public law should be supporting those other kinds of relationships that are going to be very integral to the stability of our society and our children. That's not to be judgemental about those people who are living in those kinds of relationships. There are a lot of them and that's fine. I realize some of those are committed relationships, probably more committed than mine, but it's a question whether public law should be supporting that particular version.

Q   When two people who care about each other exhibit that kind of commitment; that kind of stability within a community – they may own a home together – they may have been together ten years or twenty years– they do volunteer work, they're employed in a profession – they continue to learn – they vote, they give something back to the community – they have children – their whole life focus is toward all of the things that are in line with good strong family values; shouldn't society make some sort of room for them?

Mr. Wesolek: *There already is. If they live together for six or seven years, it's considered common law marriage. It's just as easy for them to go and get a marriage license.*

Q   What if they're homosexual and in that kind of relationship?

Mr. Wesolek: *That's a different issue entirely. Marriage has a particular definition which means man and woman and somehow children. Homosexual relationships are not part of that scheme. We feel it very important to keep the nuclear family protected by law because it's being devastated from so many directions, that it's in deep trouble. Because the family's in deep trouble, society's in deep trouble in many ways.*

Q   Then why shouldn't we do everything we can to encourage and promote people who love and care about each other, that have strong committed values, not only to each other, but to their community, their fellow man, and to the country?

Mr. Wesolek: *I think that we should. The difference comes when you make this an alternative publicly, then the message gets really changed around. Then it becomes an alternative to marriage and we don't see it as marriage.*

One of the strategic moves of Domestic Partnership is really the issue of marriage. I think that's what they're really looking at and they're looking for on a state-wide basis and to change the law which would recognize two persons, rather than a man and a woman.

Q   How did the proponents and the opposition handle themselves before the voting on this issue last year?

Mr. Wesolek: *I think it got pretty dicy at times. It's a very emotional issue, very symbolic. In the election two years ago, when it failed, we were the targets of a real campaign of hatred...threats, hate calls, graffiti, trashing the cathedral and some church services being disrupted with shouting and screaming. It wasn't a group of white heterosexuals from the suburbs. There's been a real history of militant homosexual activists. Last year there was some of that.*

We knew we were not in a popular seat. Our message was not something that San Francisco was dying to hear or would be enthusiastically received. We wanted to do it in a reasoned, civic kind of debate. We're not homophobic, we're very compassionate but believe strongly in those principles I outlined before.

Conservative right wingers were the kind of people who were against Domestic Partners. They threw up a lot of the stuff about bigotry and hatred. That was their strategy for winning politically.

Q   What can society do to make a place for homosexuals?

Mr. Wesolek: *It touches on issues like "Is society going to make homosexuality normative?" From our tradition, we say it isn't. It touches on issues like "Is it genetic?" and "Is it learned behavior?" Once society starts saying it's normative, it's like a wave you can't stop. So, more and more children see it, children who usually go through a real period of their lives in adolescence where they're going through identity question, sexually, etc. If they see it as normative, it's going to change things dramatically. It's going to mean that you're going to have a society that fully integrates a homosexual life style into it. That's what's really an issue now. That kind of sexuality would be a normative. It would be an option.*

Q   Would that necessarily mean people would choose that?

Mr. Wesolek: *No. Some will and some won't, but I think that you can certainly tilt someone who is going through a real crisis in terms of their adolescence. That certainly can happen, has happened, and does happen.*

We're guiding in a certain way that leans very heavily on a marriage being a very important element in society and that sexuality outside that relationship, whether it's heterosexual sex, or homosexual sex, or single sex, is not right.

END

Jim Robinson was a candidate for Supervisor and ran in the November 1990 election in San Francisco.

(He declined to be interviewed for this book, explaining that he has been suspicious of interviews because he has been given some bad press in the past, and that he was reluctant to be interviewed by someone he didn't personally know.)

The following was included in the Voter Information Booklet for the November 1990 Election:

Paid arguments against Proposition K

This is an attempt by the militant homosexual-dominated political establishment to use our city government to force our endorsement of perverted and illicit sexual relationships. It is a mockery of marriage. It attempts to provide the benefits of marriage without the responsibilities. It would open the door to astronomical financial costs.

Use your common sense. Vote No on K.

A vote for me is a vote against domestic partnerships and for family values.

Jim Robinson
Candidate for Supervisor

Jim Robinson's campaign slogan "Watch My Video" promoted a 30 minute video tape called "A City Divided."

The following article appeared in *The Bay Area Reporter* :

Singer Holly Near Targets Campaign

Unauthorized Footage in Anti-Prop K Video *by Dennis Conkin*

Internationally renowned entertainer Holly Near will take legal action against the Robinson for Supervisor campaign concerning its unauthorized use of her image and song in an anti-gay, anti-domestic partners videotape.

"I've just been informed that the Citizens for Common Sense campaign has been using my image and song in the campaign for Jim Robinson and against Prop K," Near told the *Bar Area Reporter*. "I am outraged. This was done without my knowledge or permission."

Historically, let it be clear that this song was written to mourn the murder of Harvey Milk and has been used and adopted by peaceful, loving people all over the world. Let the song remind us of our strengths, integrity, dignity and courage.

"May we always be singing for our lives. I support Prop K - that's for the record." Near said in a statement released by the Yes on K Committee.

Jolin Worley, Near's manager, said that use of the song and Near's image was "copyright infringement," done without permission or credit and that

Robinson had no right to distribute or sell tapes with Near on them.

The tapes are sold by Robinson for $7 a piece. The campaign has paid thousands to a video company for producing and duplicating them.

The video slams domestic partners legislation, and assails campaign manager Jean Harris, as well as public officials including Mayor Art Agnos, Assembly Speaker Willie Brown and the Rev. Cecil Williams of Glide Memorial Methodist Church.

The tape also documents last year's successful efforts by the group to defeat Prop S.

Here are excerpts from that Video Tape:

The video begins with Holly Near's song "We are gentle, angry people and we are singing for our lives. We are gay and lesbian and we are singing for our lives."

(Voices of persons speaking at a Gay and Lesbian Day Parade in San Francisco)

(Male) "We've got over 275,000 people here and they're still coming from Market St. into the Plaza area."

(Male) "Many things have happened in this country that have affected us simply because we are gay. They have affected us adversely when they should not have. AIDS is one of those crises."

(Female) "Happy Gay and Lesbian day to everybody. I love you. This has to be one of the most exciting moments in my life as a black lesbian originally from Iowa. Yes, we are everywhere.

Our specific goal includes eliminating the self-fulfilling prophecy of our invisibility as black gays and lesbians in the United States and around the world, being black advocates for social change. That means we advocate for the elimination of racism, sexism, homophobia, economic inequity, ageism, discrimination against disabled persons, AIDS mis-education, and alcohol and drug abuse. These oppressions have, for too long, disempowered both the black community and the lesbian and gay community and has separated us one from another.

We need your love, we need your support, we need all persons, all colors, all sexual orientations, all abilities, to come forth together and do away with the fear that is keeping us from actualizing our full potential so we can all stand rightfully proud."

(Voice of Willie Brown, Assembly Speaker) "I can clearly see George and Harvey smiling and looking at each other when Art got elected to the Mayorship of this town. I can see Moscone and Milk talking seriously about how to negotiate with Harry [Britt] as the new president of the Board of Supervisors. You understand that San Francisco is still the number one island of sanity and humanity in the nation."

Jim Robinson: "What does Willy Brown mean? Why is San Francisco more sane or humane than any other place in the United States? Is it because our society is so divided? Is it because pornography flourishes? Is it because we're the epicenter of AIDS or that we license parlors where mutilation takes place on other people? Because we have a growing drug problem? Because the suicide rate is so much higher here? Not only have people left their hearts in San Francisco, but many have left their bodies here... In the face of death from AIDS, the trend is to party and continue in promiscuous sexual activity. Eat, drink, and party because tomorrow, we die. Our city is in a state of denial.

I'm Jim Robinson, the candidate for Supervisor in San Francisco...I want to deal with the root causes that are dividing and destroying our city...It's part of their national agenda to pass these Domestic Partnership Ordinances all over the country and San Francisco's the key.

They're going to tell you that it doesn't cost anything. And, in a sense that's true. The ordinance itself merely provides for the registration of couples both heterosexual and homosexual as Domestic Partners. The registration fees are to be high enough to cover the costs of the program, so in reality, there are no costs. But, it creates the legal entities and the City policies are already in place to provide benefits. Nobody knows how much it is ultimately going to cost but, it will be astronomical.

However, I don't oppose the Domestic Partnership Ordinance only because of the cost. I don't think the City of San Francisco has the authority to redefine the family unit which has stood for centuries. This is a social and moral issue, not a political issue to be decided by a municipality.

...Passage of this ordinance would mean that our city would be endorsing non-marital sexual relationships. This would lay the ground work for payment of future City benefits to these non-married couples, both heterosexuals and homosexuals, thus, more costs and more promiscuity, more costs, more AIDS, more death, more costs and on and on, ad infinitum. It's time that decent, common sense citizens took control of our city again.

END

David Gilmour, 52, was the Campaign Manager against Domestic Partnership in 1990.

Q   Why did need for Domestic Partnership arise?

Mr. Gilmour: *I'm convinced that it originated with people trying to create a new standard of acceptable family life, primarily through the gay and lesbian communities. They were feeling rejection of not being able to attain that kind of status. I think that the person who wrote the original laws was a spokesperson or a legal mind or writer for that group of people.*

Q   Why the opposition?

Mr. Gilmour: *Three issues really do matter to a lot of people; the legal, the financial or the cost factor of city insurance is an unknown, and the moral concern for a redefinition of family.*

I believe that if it's going to be put on the equivalent to marriage, which it is in my mind, then it should be handled at a state level. There's a way to keep things in state levels that are absorbed by, used by, approved by, suggested by the majority of the people.

I think that the whole structure of society and families, and certainly in our American culture, has been based on the more defined traditional families. Always, there's exceptions to that. People don't disapprove of how people choose to be the exception to things, but that doesn't mean they legalize it either, and say, "Let's make them have the same benefits."

Part of the proponent mentality in the Domestic Partnership was Project 10. It was basically saying that, "10% of the students are gay and lesbian, therefore, why don't we teach and counsel and take care of these 10% through a program paid for by the taxpayers, through a program in the public schools and set up counseling on each campus. There's a handful of people who would say, "We have an agenda. This agenda will never fly if we just stick to our agenda, so why don't we make it more all inclusive?" They have an agenda for more than just Domestic Partnership.

Q   What's in the future on this issue?

Mr. Gilmour: *I believe that it is established here. I don't believe it will ever become a big deal. I believe that there's a reason that you'll see it proposed in other cities. The West Coast in general is progressive, a lot of things originate here. We have an affect on clothing styles, drama, whatever. I think because it got passed in San Francisco, that the council persons of many other cities would say it was more acceptable to do it because there's precedent set. Where before, they said, "Wait, if they can't pass that in San Francisco, I ain't going to pass it here in Iowa."*

I do believe that a lot of people in the heterosexual community are living together in a stronger sense of permanence and there's a kind of acceptability by society.

END

What the Heterosexual Domestic Partners had to say...

The following are excerpts from taped interviews
with four of the heterosexual couples
that filed for Domestic Partnership
on Valentine's Day 1991 in San Francisco City Hall.

Eleesa-37 Landscape Architect
James-39 Software Consultant

Q Why did you file for Domestic Partnership on Valentine's Day?
James: *Because we're in love. It was Valentine's Day and it seemed like a wonderful idea that San Francisco would have the concept of Domestic Partnership.*
Q How do your families feel?
Eleesa: *They were delighted. I think they would have preferred that we got married because it was something they understood. In many ways they didn't take Domestic Partnership seriously. It was one of those crazy things people did in San Francisco.*
James: *My uncle and aunt sent a congratulatory card that clearly didn't quite get it.*
Eleesa: *Hallmark didn't exactly have a printed message for Domestic Partnership.*
Q What about the opposition to Domestic Partnership?
James: *Homophobia, no question.*
Eleesa: *It's this belief in this traditional nuclear family, Mom, Dad, get married, the one correct way that people should live their lives. I think Domestic Partnership broadens what people mean by family. I think that is threatening to people who haven't thought about it very deeply.*
Q What if it were only for opposite sex couples?
James: *There would be some opposition, but not nearly as much.*
Q Did you have any other ceremony?
Eleesa: *We went ahead and had a wedding and the marriage. We filed for Domestic Partnership on Valentine's Day and then, on July 1st, my father was diagnosed with terminal cancer. I wanted a family gathering. I wanted a rallying of what family I had left. I wanted him to participate before he was gone. In no way does it diminish the Domestic Partnership. It still is an important thing to do and I'm supportive of it.*
Q How would you like to see the law?
Eleesa: *That there's a recognition that Domestic Partnership is family. Your primary mate is the person primarily responsible for you and not your family. The marriage tradition is older than Christianity. It's the oldest human ceremony. The kind of social ritual that brings a community together and cements a couple together in order to continue into the future. That ancient history is not present in a Domestic Partnership law. It doesn't have the impact that marriage has. It diminishes it for gay people. They can't participate in a commonly understood ritual.*

James: *Marriage should either be extended to all people that want it or the State should get out of the marriage business. People should be treated equally, regardless of their sexual orientation.*

Q Wouldn't it have been enough to have a Domestic Partnership celebration to bring your family together?

Eleesa: *Maybe if they were born and raised in San Francisco, it would be a commonly understood language.*

Q Had you considered marriage?

Eleesa: *We talked about it. James said it was inevitable. We bought this house, so we had made a financial commitment to each other. Maybe everybody goes through a series of increasing commitments, at least in this world.*

James: *We hadn't set a date to get married, except maybe in the abstract. It was the demise of her father that provided the catalyst for the timing.*

Eleesa: *It was a matter of when, not if.*

END

John-35 Attorney
Julie-29 Attorney

Q How long had you lived together?

Julie: *Three and one-half years. We had known each other a few months before that.*

Q Why did you file for Domestic Partnership on Valentine's Day?

John: *After we met each other, we traveled in Asia for about 18 months. We read about Domestic Partnership passing while we were out of the country. We decided that this would be a wonderful thing to do when we got back to San Francisco. Let's do it to celebrate what we've got. It was also nice to participate in something that San Francisco has and recognizes that other parts of the country don't.*

Julie: *We went down on Valentine's Day because it was the first day and it was romantic. We both wanted to recognize the relationship in some way, although we weren't ready to get married. I wanted to choose something non-traditional. I was brought up very traditionally.*

It's nice to develop your relationship at a pace that you set for yourselves instead of having the pace be dictated by other pressures. Our feelings for each have progressed and did not need some outside recognition.

John: *I don't think the legal implications were the most significant part of it. I think that the public celebration of our intimacy and our commitment was what counted.*

Q Why didn't you get engaged or married?

Julie: *It seemed that if we weren't ready at that point to get married, for whatever reasons, that this is an opportunity to some way recognize our relationship and celebrate it in a way that did not involve all the formality and energy and coordinating of families that goes into having a wedding. It was a way of recognizing it between ourselves before we did anything else.*

John: *There's different ways of celebrating or showing your public commitment and the nature of your relationship with somebody. I think marriages in this country and California fail at such a spectacular rate. To suggest that a commitment that you would call marriage is somehow more meaningful than this, would not be valid. The level of hoopla that is involved with marriage, family and big ceremony and things, at that stage, we weren't necessarily interested in. The more meaningful part of marriage or Domestic Partnership is the public announcement of your commitment.*

Q The legal benefits are different in Domestic Partnership than in marriage.

Julie: *If and when we decide to get married, I wouldn't do it because of the legal benefits that are attached to it. It would be an expression of my commitment to John. In the same way, I think the Domestic Partnership is an expression of that commitment. I certainly wouldn't feel any more or less committed by getting married than I do now.*

Q Will you get married?

John: *I wouldn't be surprised if someday we got married.*

Julie: *Until you get married, people don't necessarily view your relationship as seriously as you do. There may come a point when we say we're getting married and we want you to recognize our relationship as such, and for family, too.*

Q What would terminate your relationship?

John: *Julie's driving, very possibly. I can't think of anything else.*

Q How do you feel about living in San Francisco?

John: *I don't think we could live any other place in America.*

Q If you got married, would that change your relationship?

Julie: *Going through a formal ceremony and getting a marriage certificate doesn't say to me that anything is going to change. I don't think either one of us would feel any more of an obligation than we do now.*

John: *I'd like to think that a piece of paper with a government entry of*

*your relationship would neither, by itself, save a relationship or destroy it,
but that other things more intrinsic to the relationship would decide how it
went.*

*Maybe family pressures force couples into changing their roles because
of the label of husband and wife. We've been able to define our own
relationship because our parents and other family are thousands of miles
away. The role models that we follow are things that we've defined for
each other and are less changed by somebody else's definition.*

*I think that parents are good at sensing when their kids are happy.
There are so many miserable marriages around. If they see that their kids
are happy, I think that is the bottom line for them. Gay and lesbian
couples would be less vulnerable to falling into June and Ward
stereotypes.*

*If you count on a paper as the bedrock of your relationship, you may
not be on bedrock at all.*

END

Jeffrey-42 Importer
Mona-48 Importer

Q How long had you lived together?
Jeffrey: *Eight years, going out for nine.*
Q Why did you file for Domestic Partnership on Valentine's Day?
Mona: *We heard about Domestic Partnership and thought we'd swing by
City Hall on our way from the warehouse to the office and a car pulled out
from a place right in front of City Hall.*

*We talked about getting married and every time decided not to. We
live together, we work together, and we're together 24-hours a day.
Everybody around us is either divorced or alone.*
Jeffrey: *It's more a question of why get married. We don't have anyone
putting pressure on us. We met later in life than normal couples meet.
My other brothers are married and divorced and I'm not married and we
have the best relationship. My parents are happy, we're happy. They
don't care that we don't have a traditional marriage. Neither one of us are
very traditional or religious. Both being non-conformist enough to not
really be interested in getting married for getting married's sake, we never
have and probably never will...or maybe we will.*
Mona: *I think that it was more than just chance that we went by City
Hall. When we were about to do it, we both had this nervous question as
if we were getting married.*
Jeffrey: *We had about a day of looking at each other, reflective. To be*

*together, as long as we have, and not get married, there's a conscious
choice not to do it. This was the first visible evidence that is on paper,
framed and on the wall, which made it really special to do. It became a
lot more special to us after we did it. It meant more than we thought it
would. We realized the significance of it over the next couple of days.*
Mona: *It created, somehow, more of a bond, whatever they say marriage
does for you, aside from the bad things.*

Q   Would marriage change your relationship?
Jeffrey: *I've seen it happen to other people consistently. I think that
there's a "Father Knows Best/Donna Reed Show" structure in American
society that creates the stereotypical roles of provider, husband, and
housewife and you find yourself falling into this niche.*

   *Often, it's not who people are. They have to alter their roles to fit some
kind of silly concept of what a married couple is. Suddenly, expectations
change...now that you're my husband, you're supposed to be this...now
that you're my wife, why isn't my dinner ready? If you don't get involved
in it, then you don't have that disrupting your living. We have more than
a married relationship because all of our resources, energy, and money
from both of us have gone into us starting a business together. That's more
of a commitment in terms of time and energy than most marriages ever
are.*

Q   What have you promised each other?
Jeffrey: *To be totally honest with each other. Total communication
dictates total commitment. We wrote each other into our will as
benefactor.*

Q   What would terminate your relationship?
Jeffrey: *After all we've been through, death.*

Q   Why the opposition to Domestic Partnership?
Jeffrey: *I think it is a gay issue.*
Mona: *Certainly, there's no opposition to heterosexual couples living
together. You don't read about that everyday in the paper.*

Q   How would you like to see the law?
Jeffrey: *Something between Domestic Partnership and marriage.
Domestic Partnership had a birth here. I looked at it as a place for an
evolution of an alternative to marriage that makes a lot more sense in
helping people bond together, rather than creating the pressures that cause
people to break up. We're getting into how to reflect legally the spiritual
things that need to be dealt with. This was the first step in a process of San
Francisco leading the way in some kind of evolution of alternatives to
marriage. There are a tremendous amount of people of the same sex that
need this and should be able to have it.*

END

Ellen-44 Family Nurse Practitioner, City and County of San Francisco
David-44 Truck Driver and Political Activist

Q How long had you lived together?
Ellen: *Thirteen years. We knew each other three years before that.*
Q Why did you file for Domestic Partnership on Valentine's Day?
Ellen: *Our number reason was that one of our friends helped develop the concept of Domestic Partnership. It was partly because of our relationship with him, but also, because it meant a lot to us. It reflected our relationship more accurately than marriage. Marriage had hardly been an issue except for our mothers.*
David: *It was a special day. There was a celebration. We could have gone down any day but it wouldn't have been a celebration. It wouldn't have been publicly acknowledged.*
Ellen: *We felt amazed walking down the stairs. We were surprised. People were clapping...who are they clapping for? I wished we had invited people. It seemed a shame not to have made it more, with our friends and family.*
Q Why the opposition to Domestic Partnership?
David: *Because it legitimized non-married people in general and gay people specifically. It acknowledged and legitimized that gay people could have committed, sustained relationships and families, even though nothing material was gained. It was a political loss to the right wingers.*
Ellen: *Marriage is the only legitimate way to have a relationship. There wasn't that much of a difference between our Domestic Partnership ceremony and our marriage ceremony.*
David: *It's about morality. I think it's about right wing control of our lives.*
Q Did you get married?
Ellen: *We had to get married. In order to adopt a child in the State of California, a couple has to be married, and only heterosexual couples can be married. Our lawyer told us that if we did not get married, we would seriously endanger the adoption.*
Q Would you have gotten married otherwise?
Ellen: *No, and certainly not when we did. I don't know if we ever would have or not. We've been together so long and we're committed to each other. We did not really have a reason to be married.*
David: *Now that we're married, I am able to take advantage of the health benefits of her contract where, as a Domestic Partner, it would have cost me a lot of money.*

Ellen: *We're not religious people, so we didn't feel we were living in sin. That's one reason people get married. We're committed to each other, but people say, "Don't you want to prove your commitment?"*
David: *How can we prove it by going to some stranger who doesn't know us and says a bunch of hocus-pocus?*
Ellen: *The reasons people get married did not apply to us.*
David: *Except for a break on our income tax, but that has become less and less of an advantage.*
Ellen: *The thing that I really like about Domestic Partners is that it's very democratic and equal. Now that I'm married, I get all this mail. It's suddenly Mrs. David. I'm a feminist. You don't have to change your name. The really gut experience is being 44 and having suddenly become somebody else's name. I feel like we have a real 50/50 relationship.*

Our family was so overwhelmed by it. We just went to Juvenile Hall. We had to go through a metal detector on the way to get married. My mother was actually saying things like, "This is the biggest day of your life."

Domestic Partnership actually meant a lot more to us. It was more of an organic kind of ceremony. It really amplified the kind of relationship we have much more than marriage which is the State and certain laws applying and our families acting in these really stereotyped ways.

It's really a very powerful thing to be able to celebrate significant landmarks. Sometimes, when we reject social convention, we don't necessarily replace them with anything. We don't really have this way of celebrating and cementing what we have and letting our friends and family appreciate what we have.

That was the good part of our marriage. We had a baby shower. It gave people a chance to really appreciate us. To allow people to do that was very difficult, but it was such a good feeling. For fifteen years, we really haven't had a medium for people to be able to do that. That's the good part of why people have these things. They're necessary rituals.

I've lived within the gay community for a long time, though I'm not gay. I think on this issue of Domestic Partnership, gay people have really spearheaded it, but it has a lot of significance for straight people. I have a lot of friends and work with a lot of people who also have long-term relationships and children, and for their own reasons, never wanted to get married.

It really took this huge group of people who have no other options. They can't pass as being married. Having made the comparison between being a Domestic Partner and being married makes me realize how left out gay couples are. There's a contrast in how people treat us now that

we're married and how they treated us before, even though our
relationship hasn't changed at all. We have the privilege to make that
choice.

Q What have you promised each other?

David: *We promised to tell the truth to each other, be supportive and
work things out by talking and to be friends.*

Ellen: *Part of our vows was this quote from the anarchist that got married.
It said, "We're getting married for our own reasons and the State cannot
dictate the measure of our relationship."*

David: *We did not recognize the authority of the State in our
relationship.*

Ellen: *Then we quoted from the Song of Solomon that said "You are my
friend and my beloved."*

Q How do your families feel?

David: *There is such a marked difference in the way my mother and my
sister talk to Ellen, now that she's married and has a kid.*

Ellen: *Now, I'm the wife. Now, they know who I am.*

David: *Sometimes, they didn't talk to her. There is so much more
warmth and extroversion going on now after the kid and the marriage.*

Ellen: *Before, it was like we didn't exist. We weren't a relationship
even though we've been together all these years, much more than any of
our other relatives going on their third marriages. Actually, I would have
preferred to keep the relationship with just Domestic Partnership.*

David: *They thought Domestic Partnership was weird. A few days after
we got married, we had a luncheon for some friends and our family to
acknowledge our marriage. Certain members of my family have always
made it clear to me that marriage is real important, so I was going to let
them in on it because that's what they really wanted to have happen.
Since then, their response to us is different. It's more warm and more
open. They will call and talk. My mother hardly ever used to call and talk
to Ellen.*

Ellen: *Everything's fallen into place. The world is as they understand it.
Our relationship is legitimate now.*

David: *They've always had doubts, I guess, because they couldn't define
it. Now we're married. We've proven to them that we're for real. Even
though we each have more than one cousin that has been married two or
three times. There's so much divorce in our families and the people we
know, it's ridiculous.*

Ellen: *David's family is a conventional Catholic family. You have to go
back generations to find real social convention in my family.*

Q Tell me about your child.

David: *Anarose, what a dream. A dream come true.*

Ellen: *Almost two years ago, I found out that I couldn't have a baby. We had been planning for quite a while and putting it off. I always assumed I could easily get pregnant. So, we explored our options and decided on adoption.*

David: *This is called Open Adoption, it's very structured. The adopting parties know each other in some way and establish some kind of relationship which could go on for the rest of our life and the child's life.*

Ellen: *It puts a lot more control in the hands of the birth mother. Some friends told us about an adolescent that was pregnant and wanted to give the baby up for adoption. We contacted her and got a lawyer. She lived with us until after the birth. We became pals. She hasn't decided if she will have continued involvement with Anarose. We hope so.*

Q What would terminate your relationship?

David: *Death.*

Q How would you like to see the law?

Ellen: *I'd like people's relationship to be legitimate, period...by their own definition. I don't think their sexual orientation or their religion should matter. I think couples should have the same benefits, legal and cultural, regardless of who they are. Why not make it equal for everyone who had a relationship?*

END

What the Gay and Lesbian Domestic Partners had to say...

The following are excerpts from taped interviews
with over forty of the homosexual couples
that filed for Domestic Partnership on Valentine's Day 1991
in San Francisco City Hall.

Those interviewed included:

Gael-35 Human Resources Manager for a Law Firm
Denise-30 Director of Registration Services for a Meeting Planner

John-35 Administrative Assistant in the Banking Industry
Richard-37 Personnel Recruiter in the Banking Industry

David-45 University Administrative Assistant in Accounting
David-40 Molecular Biologist and Geneticist

Lori-28 Waitress
Anita-35 Customer Service Representative

Jack-60   Night Supervisor
Harry-63 Semi-retired

Bert-45 AIDS Counselor
Gwynn-28   Graphic Designer

William-62 Retired United States Government Employee
Roderick-57 Administrative Assistant of Marketing

Deena-23 Customer Service Manager - Computer Operations
Gwendolyn-26 Legal Secretary

Tony-39 Production Manager
Joel-47 Self-Employed House Painter

Steve-45 Distinguished Engineer
Eric-29 Horticulturist

Hugh-46 Psychiatric Nurse
David-40 Nurse

Brent-38 Market Specialist
Wade-34 Compensation Analyst

Dan-40 Registered Psychiatric Nurse
Steve-49 Freelance Entertainment/Feature Writer

Helene-39 Attorney
Kit-39 Software Engineer

Lauren-29 Account Manager
Jane-29 Customer Service Manager

Joan-24 Administrative Assistant/Cartoonist
Louise-28 Freelance Editor

Brad-30 Accountant
Carl-46 Retired from the Transportation Industry

Wally-37 Architect
Richard-28 Truck Driver

Jay-41 Realtor
Kenneth-45 Technical Specialist in Telecommunications

Anne-38 Certified Public Accountant
Simone-52 High School Teacher

Phillip-27 Treasury Analyst
Stephen-35 Bookkeeper

Rachel-30 Security Officer
Joan-45 Librarian

Lynn-38 Marketing Researcher
Jackie-40 Research Consultant

Adria-Ann-43 Attorney
Kris-26 Clinical Social Worker

Wood-45 Administration, Mills College
Larry-45 Human Rights Commission of San Francisco

Kenneth-32 Display Designer
Steven-30 Hair Cutter

Hugh-51 Chief Deputy, County Coroner's Office
Richard-34 Dentist

Stephanie-48   Psychotherapist
Jeanette-37   Obstetrician/Gynecologist

James-41   Graphics Production
Jeffrey-38   Information Analyst

Kevin-37   Psychotherapist
Dan-37   Psychotherapist

Chuck-38   AIDS Educator
Steve-37   High School Teacher

Annette-32   Medical Administrative Analyst
Sandy-35   Medical Receptionist

Otto-60   Retired from the Insurance Industry
Dick-60   Retired Technician

Alice-40   Health Worker and Phone Installer
Christmas-42   Registered Nurse and Lay Midwife

John-33 Purchaser for a Wholesale Art Company
James-29 Unemployed Shipping Clerk

Katherine-40 Self-Employed Convention Manager
Darien-47   Marketing and Advertising

Ben-32 On-line Manager in the Computer Industry
Todd-27 Sociology Student

Chris-26 Custom Leather Garments
Richard-30 Assistant Manager of a Video Store

Lee-33 Field Service Representative for a Computer Company
Chris-33 Scientific Quartz Glass Blower

Jane-49 Presbyterian Minister
Coni-39 Pastor of a Metropolitan Community Church

Marty-32   Paramedic, SF Dept. of Public Health
Susan-33   Paramedic, SF Dept. of Public Health

Why did you file for Domestic Partnership on Valentine's Day?

Denise 30   *Well, we considered ourselves married. We've been together almost six and one-half years now. It just gave us a little ceremony to go with it and some public recognition. It's great to have this piece of paper that we have stuck on the wall in the hallway so everyone who comes in knows of our attachment to each other. We're not just a couple of people who are living together.*

For straight people, divorce is a messy thing, so a lot of people stay married for better or for worse. The image of gay people is that we just mess around and it's not that way, it's a committed relationship, love. We had announcements made up and we mailed them to most of our family. I wanted them to know. My brothers have all been married at least once, some of them twice.

Gael 35   *One of the big things was, that it made some things less hidden.*

———————————❤———————————

Richard 37   *It was just something we wanted to be a part of. As a gay couple, we wanted to associate ourselves with a community of gay couples and acknowledge that not only are we a lot of individuals out there, but we also make up a sizable community.*

John 35   *It was the next step. It was a way for San Francisco and the rest of the country to recognize that we are registered as partners.*

———————————❤———————————

David 40   *It's something that shows people that you have a relationship. It gives it a little more substance. You've actually gone out in public and said you have a relationship.*

David 45   *I did it more to validate that the City, the State, and the Government should be allowing this. Ideally, we would like to be married and be able to file joint tax returns and have all the legal status of being married. We did it to encourage the politicians to move to further steps. There are things that come up, like parental leave from work, family bereavement leave or sick leave that are specifically for family members only and do not include non-family members. The Domestic Partnership document may help.*

We both took the day off from work, spent a very pleasant day together and had a nice meal. A month later, we had a large party and invited all of our friends over. It was for our 15th anniversary and to celebrate our Domestic Partnership.

❤

Jack 60   *At our age, health is a consideration. There is the possibility that we might get into some type of hospital where they would insist that only next of kin could visit. At some later date, a law may be passed where Harry might be able to get my social security or vise versa. I didn't need a piece of paper to tell that Harry and I loved each other.*

❤

Gwynn 28   *We were already planning on getting married later in the year, on our two year anniversary, with a marriage ceremony we had invented ourselves. We have the pictures and video to prove it.   We both felt very strongly about Domestic Partnership and being visible, and were proud of ourselves for it.*

❤

Deena 23   *We had worked so hard for the measure and because we're serious about our relationship and would like to be able to get married.*
Gwen 26   *It seemed like an historic moment that we wanted to take part in.*

❤

Tony 39   *Because we could. Up until then, there was no way to recognize our relationship in a legal sense. We did feel an obligation to the gay community to go down to City Hall and say "Here we are, we've been living together, we love each other and we want the same rights as everybody else."*
Joel 47   *It was an historical event. There is no way that we would not have done it.*
Tony   *Living here in San Francisco, you tend to forget what the rest of the world is like. When Joel was in the hospital, I had absolutely no problem being at his bedside the whole time he was there and after hours. It's not like we went down to City Hall to have that right, because I don't feel that we've been denied it. We have been denied health insurance and other things. We know where we live.   We feel very lucky about that.*
Joel   *We've never been in the closet. Going down to City Hall was not coming out in any way.*

❤

Steve 45   *It was something that was essential to us. We knew we were committed to each other for life, however long that might be, and any recognition we could get from the State for that was of importance.*
Eric 29   *It was important for us to have our relationship recognized in San Francisco, which I call home now.*

———————❤———————

Hugh 46   *It was a way of documenting that we have a commitment to each other. On a political level, gays and lesbians for a long time have been invisible and we need to be not invisible if we want to have change. On the emotional level, we were making a statement to each other. I was kind of nervous, actually, on the day of the ceremony. I hadn't thought much about it before that. I woke up kind of anxious, the old bride/groom syndrome.*

David 40   *Because we could. If we could get married, we would, but we can't and this is just a step in that direction. I feel that in a way, we're now recognized, but in a second class relationship. It's still not the same, legally, as marriage.*

———————❤———————

Brent 38   *To support the passage of that legislation. We thought it was an important social statement to make. I think that we need to recognize alternative families because they certainly exist.*

———————❤———————

Dan 40   *It was a public validation of our relationship, a step toward gay couples actually being married.*

———————❤———————

Steve 49   *We wanted to be one of the first group and try to boost the numbers.*

———————❤———————

Helene 39   *Domestic Partnership in practicality doesn't mean a lot. If a couple registers, it doesn't give them the same legal rights that a heterosexual married couple would have. It does give people a few rights, such as visiting people in the hospital or bereavement leave in some cases. It's more of a symbolic gesture of showing that there are gay and lesbian couples out there that do have committed relationships and that probably would, if the opportunity was present legally, get married. Ideally, if we could get the same kind of benefits that a married, heterosexual couple would have, it would give us a lot of practical, legal rights that we don't have now, like getting on the other person's insurance. I think the emotional dynamics of our relationship are already equivalent to what a heterosexual couple would have.*

———————❤———————

Lauren 29   *It was romantic.*
Jane 29   *It was Lauren's idea. Despite the fact that I was the radical lesbian in the family, I didn't want the Government to have my name. As the backlash has increased over the 80's, I was very hesitant to do this, but*

Lauren really pushed. It was the first opportunity for us to get married and fear shouldn't enter into the equation of not doing it.

---❤---

Richard 28   *To take part in an historic event.*

Wally 37   *What it meant is, that I have faith in our relationship with each other. I have faith that we can grow together. I'm committed to working with Richard to make a relationship rather than having the ceremony be the commitment, or an exchange of rings be the commitment. I'm committed to work with him to try to make a nice life together, rather than I'm going to be married to him "until death do us part." It was an investment in potential.*

Richard   *It was the closest we could get to a marriage of any sort. One of the reasons that people see and generalize that the gay community doesn't have serious commitments, is that there's nothing that binds you together. In a marriage a man and woman will fight and tend to try to work things out because they've got to go through the divorce and the settlement. In a gay relationship, that isn't there. It's too easy to pick up and go your separate ways, so I saw it as something to bind you together, a base to work you through hard times.*

Wally   *We fight and have disagreements and at some point in the anger, you remember or the ring flashes, and you remember that you've made a commitment downtown at City Hall.*

---❤---

Anne 38   *Because it was the first day allowed and it was the first legal time that we could be recognized. In many ways, our filing was less a commitment statement, because we had already made that, and more of a political statement.*

---❤---

Steve 35   *It was the first day that we could do that. It was symbolic. We consider ourselves married. One of the things we insisted on, was that we had a wedding, not a Holy Union, because the laws do not recognize that we are married. We do and we want everyone else to. We have our certificate that we got from the wedding framed and on the wall with our Domestic Partnership Certificate.*

One other thing that we did, was file with the State of California to be held in an unincorporated, non-profit association. We've done everything that we can do as far as outwardly signing up and registering our relationship.

---❤---

Rachel 30 *It was political.*

Joan 45 *Because it was Valentine's Day, which has a certain sentimental value. It's a nicer day to get married than most days.*

❤

Jackie 40 *Valentine's Day is the day that we designate as our anniversary. It was a way of having it become a formal anniversary. It was also a political step toward recognition of non-traditional families, especially as it relates to health benefits and other important economic issues. On one hand, I feel empowered by having the opportunity to pay somebody $35.00 to put our names on a piece of paper and at the same time recognize how surface the gesture is. It feels very sad.*

Lynn 38 *It's the first level of visibility as a family unit.*

❤

Ken 32 *That was the first day and we wanted to make a political statement about something we need to support. For us, it's another step in confirming our relationship.*

Steve 30 *My feeling about marriage is, that it's not necessary to have that piece of paper to have a committed relationship. Making a stand socially was important for us. Ma and Pa in Iowa can look at that piece of paper and relate to it, it's something that validates the relationship, like a marriage license would for them.*

Ken *I look at it as a stepping stone to something more in the future.*

❤

Richard 34 *We wanted to make a statement that our relationship is just as valid as anybody else's.*

❤

Stephanie 48 *It was symbolic. It was Valentine's Day, the first day. It hasn't changed anything, it was a formality. It was less of a personal, emotional thing and more of a group emotion thing happening that day.*

I was against any kind of ceremony because I thought that was aping the patriarchy. I had been married before and divorced and found that a difficult, oppressive relationship. Domestic Partnerships are relationships based on equality. Gay people and lesbians getting married in the traditional marriage sense never appealed to me. This was an opportunity to make a statement, but also to make it in a way that was very different than a traditional wedding. Marriage is a tradition steeped in religion and culture and Domestic Partnership is a legal vehicle.

Jeanette 37 *It was more of a political thing. In committed relationships, partners should be able to get insurance benefits, death benefits and retirement benefits. I think Domestic Partnership is the beginning of the change.*

❤

James 41   *We wanted to support that kind of legislation and thinking.*

❤

Kevin 37   *I wanted to do something more public. We took Sarah, our daughter.*

Steve 37   *We've always celebrated Valentine's Day. We thought we might as well seize the opportunity and tie the knot.*

Personally, I don't know if I were heterosexual, if I would get married. I went down there as a political statement. Personally, I could have done without it.

❤

Chuck 38   *I was probably a little more romantic about it. When we did get the piece of paper that day, it was very meaningful. I realized its historical and political importance. That's why I supported the initiative in the first place and why I wanted to be there to do it. It's important, now that we have this, that it be taken advantage of and we prove it to be worthwhile and a success. That's the only way it will spawn more of the same in other cities.*

It changed how each of us personally relate to the relationship. Now, in my view, it's got a different slant to it. To see my name on paper was a validation and approval by a city agency. All of a sudden, the relationship had some meaning on a broader level.

❤

Annette 32   *Although we had also made plans to have a religious ceremony for our family and friends, this was the first opportunity that presented itself where we could have public recognition, and participate in a very historic moment for the City and for the Country for opening up Domestic Partnership.*

It's been hard for our parents, mine more so than Sandy's, to accept the fact that we're together and that we're in love and that love means that we're going to be together for a very long time, if not forever. To register and make a public statement was very important for our families, as will be a religious ceremony, when we have that. It lets them know that there's another perspective on thinking about lesbianism or homosexuality. There's other people out there who think it's really a great thing that two people can find one another in the world and be together.

❤

Otto 60   *It was the first opportunity we had to acknowledge our relationship to others.*

Dick 60   *It was a very moving experience. I'm sorry we didn't do* *something sooner. It improved my own self-image and feelings. I recognized feelings about the commitment and the relationship that I might have had all along, but didn't recognize.*

Otto   *It made us feel that much better about ourselves.*

Dick   *It's sort of an extension of coming out. For many years, I identified Otto as my partner and left it open to people to make whatever interpretation they wanted. People who were uncomfortable with thinking of me as being gay could choose to think of me as being in a business partnership with Otto. Now, I identify myself as Otto's partner but I say "We're Domestic Partnership #105."*

---❤---

Christmas 42   *We worked so hard on that campaign. It was political and very emotional. I always say that the personal is political, that everything you do in your personal life affects things. It's saying what you believe, if you live your life right. I worked so hard for other people's rights for so many years. I'm a lesbian and I work in women's reproductive health care and I have no children. I help women get abortions and birth control, understanding it and explaining it to them. I've helped people with civil rights stuff and worked with AIDS. This was the first thing I worked on that directly affected me and was positive.*

Alice 40   *I was born here, I've grown up here, I've gone to school here, I work here. I keep on hearing about my classmates from high school, that are all married, and they have these rights and things. When is it my turn? I'm a good person. This is somebody I really love and why can't I go down to City Hall and say, "Hey, I want to get old with this person." Why can't I do that? That's why I went down.*

---❤---

John 33   *I have worked really hard on the Proposition K last year. It was the victory celebration that day.*

James 29   *During the whole campaign, I didn't know if it was such a great idea to have Domestic Partnership. I didn't know what my status with social security would be if somebody else signed up to say that they would be responsible for my rent and food. I was getting payments for disability.*

John   *He was working with ACT UP at the same time. They weren't sure if they really wanted to endorse it. Not everybody knew exactly everything it covered. The only thing it actually covered was basic shelter and food.*

---❤---

Katherine 40   *We were engaged on Valentine's Day in 1982 and we* *are sentimental. I think that this is an important civil right. Many people fought long and hard to enact Domestic Partnership and I felt a responsibility to go down and take advantage of it. We wanted to stand up and be counted. We are a gay family and we are publicly registered and recognized as this societal unit.*

❤

Todd 27   *It was a political statement. It's important that lesbians and gays have access to the same benefits as the straight community. I see this as a stepping stone.*

Ben 32   *I felt that we had made this commitment already and that this was just the legal stamp. So, for me doing it the first day was to share in the celebration of something that we'd worked for.*

❤

Chris 26   *On Valentine's Day, I got down to City Hall at 5:00 a.m. in the morning because I wanted to be first in line and I was. Until about 8:00 a.m., there was nobody else that had showed up.*

Richard 30   *Which is about what time I arrived, because I slept late. Chris is more politically inclined than I am and I am more inclined to sleep.*

In many ways, I did it because Chris was really excited about it. I liked the idea, but it wasn't that big of a deal. The more it's gone on, the more important it's becoming to me. I was committed to Chris long before we ever registered for Domestic Partnership. It was more like a public acknowledgment by other people. I didn't need it. I think Chris needs it more than I do.

Chris   *It was real important to me because I knew that there were so many other gay and lesbian people in the country that were going to see this and it would give them some spark of hope, some realization that their relationships were valid and that people did respect those relationships. I was really proud to be a part of it.*

Q   How did you feel to be the first to register?

Chris   *Speechless. I was kind of numb.*

Richard   *There were cameras everywhere and they were all surrounding us. We were a little stunned at first.*

❤

Chris 33   *Because it was horribly cute and romantic to be there on the first day and on Valentine's Day. It's a statement of commitment.*

Lee 33   *It was political. I wanted to support that step, hoping, of course, there will be other steps.*

❤

Jane 49   *We went down to be in solidarity with the community and to participate in a spiritual service that we were asked to be a part of as Minister and Pastor. In going down to do that, it was then that we were really moved to go and do it.*

Coni 39   *It was a major happening for gay and lesbian people in the country and certainly in the Bay Area. We participated in an interfaith ceremony on the steps outside.*

———————————❤———————————

Marty 32   *Because we wanted to be legally committed to each other.*

Susan 33   *As close to legally recognized.*

Marty   *If California recognized lesbian and gay marriages, we would do that. We're willing to take that responsibility for each other.*

Susan   *Filing Domestic Partnership made me feel more committed, like I was taking that step beyond.*

How did it feel to walk down the stairs of City Hall?

Gwen 26   *It was high camp. The couples would come down the stairs and they'd read over the microphone, "Here's David and Michael and they've been together for 35 years." That's not very frivolous.*

Deena 23   *Some of the straight couples, and straight couples with children that came down the steps, got a lot more applause because they were there. Everybody had assumed that it was going to be just a gay and lesbian marriage and it wasn't. It was neat to see straight people were going to use it as well.*

Gwen   *I took it as a sign of support.*

❤

Jane 29   *I was nervous as heck. I thought we were going to trip. It was incredibly validating just to hear our names and walk down the stairs. It was the closest thing to that real wedding feeling.*

Lauren 29   *I gave Jane a wedding band.*

❤

Joan 24   *It was really nice. It was the kind of support that heterosexual couples get from their families, extended families, friends and relatives. When they get married, passersby even applaud them in their relationship.*

❤

Brad 30   *I felt wonderful. I felt elated walking down the stairs and having people applaud and having acceptance.*

Carl 46   *It was like a receiving line after a wedding. There was a lot of affirmation that you're okay and the relationship is okay and it stands and we applaud you. I didn't enter the relationship to get anything from the City, the State, the Federal Government, or Brad. I had his love and companionship anyway. Other than having it registered there and knowing that it exists, it doesn't do anything.*

I can recall some nervousness about it. I don't often make a statement about our relationship when I'm out in public. I tend to withdraw and become very prudish in displaying my emotions. Once I got there and talked to people and saw the others that were involved, I began to understand what was really happening. The two dozen red tulips Brad brought really helped.

Brad   *I got wedding bands on Carl's birthday. They will engrave them for us with our initials and the date we met, or Valentine's Day 1991.*

❤

Wally 37   *There were all these people standing down below and clapping for everybody as they walked down.*

Richard 28   *It wasn't just small groups clapping for people that they knew, everyone was clapping for everyone.*

Wally   *It was like bucking the conservative morality in the nation. To stand at the bottom and watch all the other couples come down and to see these gay couples who had been together 20 and 30 years, gave me faith that we can make it that long.*

Richard   *There were couples that had been together longer than probably 50% of the marriages in the country.*

Wally   *The role models that are publicized in gay society are not married couples, they are these big, hot sex studs and macho body builder types. The role models for gay marriage are not real clear.*

Richard   *That's because all the role models do exactly what we do. They sit at home and get videos on Saturday night.*

❤

Jay 41   *I could have died. It was a good feeling, but I was nervous. It was stage fright. The stairs are so commanding, I felt like royalty. Everybody was applauding...and the support. We went early in the morning and registered. We pulled up on a motorcycle, had our suits on, and our boutonnieres with the rainbow flag. We weren't even off the bike and somebody walked by and said congratulations.*

Ken 45   *I liked it. It was a sense of community with all these people supporting me.*

❤

Anne 38   *Proud.*

❤

Kris 26   *It was exhilarating. They made City Hall for us that day, to be cared for and acknowledged for what we were doing and who we were. It took courage, not only to go through the registration, but then to come back and go down the steps. It was so public. It's still a struggle to be that open about our relationship. To have everybody else there saying the same thing felt like a once in a lifetime experience.*

Adria-Ann 43   *It was so much more than either of us had expected. It really felt like being part of the community in a very special way. We exchanged rings and vows at the bottom of the stairs.*

Kris   *I felt compelled, from the minute it passed, to register because I wanted to send a message to the City, and to other cities that will work on legislation similar to it, that not only did we fight to get it, and get it, but that we are going to use it. We're going to tell the City that we deserve the* same things that other families get. It's discrimination to only offer benefits to people that are in heterosexually sanctioned relationships and not to people who've made other decisions or choices about their relationships. It's basically unequal compensation for the same work, based on my sexuality.

Adria-Ann *In many ways, our relationship is the same as people who get married. We have an emotional bond as a couple, as a family. We care for each other, we've made a commitment. If you look at the family in political or economic terms, as the unit that keeps the whole capitalist system functioning, we fit right in there, too. We function the same way. If it walks like a family, smells like a family, looks like a family, it is. To narrowly define the responsibilities that come with forming that unit to only people of the opposite sex is wrong.*

***

Larry 45 *I felt wonderful. I was holding hands with Wood. We kissed at the top of the stairs. Our names were announced. I was so proud to be seen with him as his partner, his lover. It felt like the culmination of years and years of work to make this happen.*

Wood 45 *I had a hard time keeping back the tears of joy. It was this beautiful affirmation of this kind love, which I know is a wonderful kind of love, and society was finally saying, "Well, I guess it is all right."*

***

Sandy 35 *I lived it. I floated down those steps. I was born and raised in San Francisco, so I've been to City Hall a million times and I've often thought how much fun it would be to go down those steps and have all that attention.*

Annette 32 *We had purchased wedding rings and had them engraved. My ring says, "Forever, Sandy, 2-14-91" and Sandy's says, "Forever, Annette, 2-14-91." After filling out our form and having it stamped by the City Clerk that day, we made a few very simple promises to one another.*

***

Christmas 42 *I felt my heart expanding in my chest. I felt like we were glowing with a big heart shape bubble around us. I knew there were a lot of people there, but I just felt like this was private. It was ours.*

***

Ben 32 *It took forever to go down the stairs. It was like the high school graduation march or the college thing. Everyone's cheering you on. It's over in a flash, but it seems like a long moment. Long moments are things you can treasure.*

Todd 27 *It was really joyful. We were nervous and smiling at each other.*

---❤---

Chris 33   *I wasn't present at that moment. My body was there and she was kissing it before we descended the stairs, but I was nowhere in the room. I was just out of my mind.*

Lee 33   *I was quite thrilled. I had taken a clue from someone else I'd seen who had kissed their partner before they went down. It felt so wonderful to just touch her cheek and kiss her in public. It was a wonderful sense, bigger than any feeling that I have a word for. Yet, walking down the stairs, I felt the same thing I feel when I'm walking through a suburban mall, "Oh my god, I'm out in public!" and there was just a touch of fear to that. But everyone down there was smiling and clapping, whether they were gay or straight. They were for it and it was a safe place.*

Chris   *Our certificate was already in a frame and I was holding it. We filed in the morning at 9:30 a.m., then went to have it framed at 10:00 a.m., and then went back down for the ceremony at 3:00 p.m.*

Lee   *The worst fear was that a copy would be just so insignificant. The original was right there. My gosh, let's get this under glass!*

---❤---

Coni 39   *I thought that it was going to be just another nice thing we were doing but it really proved to be exceedingly powerful for both of us. As we moved closer to being the two at the top of the stairs, my heart started pounding more. When do you ever get that chance to stand at the top of the stairs, have your names announced, walk down fifty or a hundred stairs, have three or four-hundred people clapping at the bottom for you and your relationship? When you're lesbian or gay, that doesn't happen. The support in society, in your own birth family, generally is not there. It was totally exhilarating.*

Here were lesbian and gay people who have traditionally been locked out of the mainstream, locked out of government, locked out of even consideration from government, let alone consideration from religious establishments and we were in the rotunda of City Hall, hardly a place, at least in San Francisco, that more represented the government of the Bay Area and this was our day. That was so empowering.

Jane   *It was a huge honor. People were clapping when so much of the world is not.*

Was there any other ceremony to celebrate your commitment?

Gael 35   *We opened a joint checking account.*
Denise 30   *We did buy rings and gave each other rings.*
Gael   *That was about three or four years after we began living together. We got the idea when the first Domestic Partnership was being introduced and we felt sure that it was going to pass and we would get rings. It didn't pass and we got rings anyway.*

———————————❤———————————

John 35   *One of the first things we did was celebrate our month anniversary with friends just because it was fun to do. For our one year anniversary we exchanged wedding bands. It was the first material kind of a discussion about a commitment. The other things (wills etc.) have evolved over the past seven years.*
Richard 37   *This was new to me. I'm learning how important it is to express how you're feeling. I've learned, that because you love someone and care about them doesn't mean that they know what you're feeling.*

———————————❤———————————

Anita 35   *We had a Holy Union a year ago and that was great for ourselves, our family, and friends. It was in the Metropolitan Community Church and we took vows to love and respect each other.*
Lori 28   *It's the same vows that you have in a wedding.*
Anita   *I have traditional values. It was a choice of ours. We didn't have to do it, but we wanted to, because we're just like everybody else.*
Lori   *Every one of our friends came, about 110 people. Anita's whole side of the family, no one from my family. About a month later I felt, "Now I know what marriage is." When you fight, you just can't walk away. We're married and we have to work it out.*
Anita   *I felt like I grew a little bit. That was in August, then in February we filed Domestic Partnership.*
Lori   *We got a document of Holy Union, but it is not recognized by the City. It was another binding, another trying to get closer to be completely legalized, and also, to have down as much as possible on paper, that we promise to be together for the rest of our lives. My parents do not agree with my life-style. If anything were to happen, they would probably come in and take everything.*
Anita   *I would lose all rights to her. They would package her up and ship her away and I would never have any contact whatsoever. It's another step for us to secure our relationship, not so much that we need it,*

but just so people outside of us know it and they're not going to tamper with us.

Lori   *It's another part of saying we're married, we're a couple and we plan on being together for the rest of our lives. We did something that not that many people will ever be able to do or maybe someday everyone will. We were one of the first to do it and that's really a wonderful thing.*

❤

Bert 45   *We had a cowboy/Jewish wedding for two hundred people.*

❤

William 62   *We went for the family registry in Washington, D.C.*

❤

Gwen 26   *We mixed our books together on the book shelves. She's been my friend for six years. By the time we got together, we were so close already, it was really easy. We already had the trust and communication. We still want to have a Holy Union in addition to Domestic Partnership.*

Deena 23   *It's as close to a wedding as you can get as a same sex couple.*

❤

Joel 47   *No. Our families have been accepting our relationship.*
Tony 39   *It was love at first sight.*

❤

Wade 34   *We remember our anniversary every year. We haven't had a ceremony before, because there wasn't a recognizable form to do that.*

Brent 38   *No, it evolved. When we got together, it was a phase of infatuation. You didn't think of it as being a lifetime commitment at all. We were in school at the time.*

Wade   *Four or five years into our relationship, it was very clear that it was a lifetime commitment.*

❤

Steve 49   *No, Domestic Partnership was the only thing. We belong to Metropolitan Community Church and have talked about having a Holy Union.*

❤

Kit 39   *We got married in our church, which is a Unitarian Universalist Church, three months after we moved in together. We had a ceremony with a minister. Parts of our families came and our friends.*

❤

Jane 29   *Domestic Partnership was the first ceremony.*
Lauren 29   *On our fifth anniversary, someone gave us a surprise party.*

♥

Richard 28 *We exchanged rings on Valentine's Day.*

♥

Simone 52 *We had a Holy Union six years ago. Our families attended and two hundred friends. Our parents were there to support us. Anne's siblings, and my older daughters were there. We weren't quite sure where to celebrate the reception, so we decided we would capture these people for four hours, going up and down the Bay on the Red and White Fleet [cruise boat]. We were going to have straight people and gay people, we were going to have conservative people and it would be very interesting.*

♥

Steve 35 *Yes. I asked him, "What does getting married mean to you?" and he said, "Rings and vows and a wedding with guests and cake and a reception...the whole nine yards."*
Phillip 27 *So, that's what we did.*
Steve *I told him I wouldn't marry him until I got an engagement ring and a week later I had a diamond earring.*
Phillip *We were married in a very traditional ceremony, we even have a wedding album. There were three hundred invited guests. Everything was very formal, very traditional from the invitations to the wedding party being in tuxedos. We had a ring bearer. Family and friends came in from all over the country.*
Steve *His brother stood up with him as his best man, my brother stood up with me. It was very exciting.*

♥

Wood 45 *We went to San Gregorio Beach. There were just the two of us. We wrote our own vows and exchanged them. It was a stormy day, but it wasn't raining. We had a sea gull as our witness.*
Larry 45 *We had each prepared the vows in advance, but didn't share them until that moment.*
Wood *We had a reception a couple of weeks later and invited all our friends and had a cake.*

♥

Steve 30 *No. We had legal documentation of our relationship within the first year. Through an attorney, we have durable powers of attorney drawn up, living wills and living together agreements. We had to consciously go out and pay $5,000 to get us legal documentation that will get us as close as possible to marriage.*

♥

Hugh 51 *We exchanged rings.*

♥

Kevin 37   *We had a private exchange of rings six years ago.*

♥

Alice 40   *At the [1987] March on Washington, we were married with two thousand couples in front of the IRS Building. It was a protest about the fact that there was no way for lesbian and gay people to be married. We had ministers and we exchanged rings. We made the rings that we exchanged.*
Christmas 42   *It was non-denominational, more spiritual. It wasn't legal but in half the states in the country I'm illegal just because I'm a lesbian.*
Alice   *We came back to our family and felt there was something missing. We had a reception a month later.*
Christmas   *We had some friends that had gone to Washington with us, but a lot of people we knew were sick. Some people were dying that were here in San Francisco. We wanted a way to celebrate life. We had all been going to a lot of funerals. For our reception, we made this big lavender, satin heart that said "Christmas and Alice Celebrate Love" on one side and on the other side it said "Love Makes a Family."*

♥

James 29   *Yes, kind of a pagan ceremony just between the two of us to do a ritual of binding. You just burn some incense and some candles and you try to focus on what you want to be and become and your love for each other. It's really informal. It has no religious connection.*

♥

Katherine 40   *We had a beautiful Holy Union Ceremony out in our back yard. It was about the most beautiful day in our lives. It was a sunny, beautiful afternoon filled with flowers and music and we wrote our own ceremony and vows. It was homey and intimate.*
Darien 47   *The guests were quite a cross-section of our friends and families. We had exchange of vows and rings. We had best ladies at our sides. We had the slicing of the cake and feeding each other the piece and the garter and the first dance.*
Katherine   *It wasn't an expensive or elaborate affair, but it was one that people have referred to over the years as having been a meaningful personal experience for each person that was there.*

♥

Ben 32   *We exchanged rings very early on when we realized that we were committed to each other.*

♥

Richard 30   *We hyphenated our names, and that was a big deal for me. We did it legally. We have also registered with the state as a non-profit* association as a family.

Chris 26 *So, legally, we are recognized by the State of California as a family.*

Richard *To hyphenate our names wasn't really a ceremony, but it's one more progressive step. When you get married, there's no question about it. With Domestic Partnership, people still question people's commitment to one another. We're doing various things so people really do understand we are totally committed.*

Chris *Gay relationships, by history, are just so easy to terminate anyway. If you're married, you've got the legal papers and you've changed your name. I don't want to be accused of trying to imitate heterosexual marriage, but I do think that there are some aspects of it that are positive. I think sharing our names is real important for me. I didn't take his name and he didn't take mine, we took each other's.*

Richard *It's not like either one of us is losing anything, we're both gaining.*

———————❤———————

Marty 32 *Yes, we did a Holy Union on May 18, 1991 up in the Redwoods. It was actually a picnic area and we transformed it. It had amphitheater seating and a big barbecue that we made into an altar. We covered it with plywood and white sheets. We had balloons and champagne. We had two wine glasses and a special box that Sue's mom had given to her with our wedding rings in it set up on the altar with flowers. We had forty of our closest friends. My mom came out from New York. For the reception, we rented the Hornblower Yacht and went out and had a three hour Bay cruise and danced.*

Susan 33 *Then, we went on a honeymoon to a women's bed and breakfast in Mendocino County. Jane Spahr, of the Metropolitan Community Church, performed the service. We met with Jane five or six different times before that. We wrote our own vows. She gave us homework so we could learn about each other and she incorporated all of that into the service. At the ceremony she talked about Marty and I, what kind of people we were and how we had gotten together. Our best friends stood up for us. It was wonderful.*

Marty *We did a vow together over an open flame which is a Buddhist tradition.*

Susan *Our Holy Union was to me a marriage, even though it wasn't legally recognized. It changed us for the better. It made us feel as though we really had made a commitment to each other, that if things got rough, that one of us wouldn't just bail out and say, "This isn't going to work, see you later." It's recognized between us and it's recognized by someone of greater power.*

What have you promised to each other?

John 35   *This is the relationship of my life. It is like a marriage. I'm going to be there for Richard and he's going to be there for me in sickness and in health and when things are good and when things are not so good. We've proven that over the last eight years.*

---❤---

David 40   *All of each other and our lives.*
David 45   *I think, until death do us part.*
David 40   *At the start, you say these things and you hope that they're real, but I think it develops and it evolves. At the very start it's a honeymoon.*
David 45   *Finally, when Domestic Partnership passed and was signed, I got down on my knees and asked David if he would be willing to be my Domestic Partner. He said ,"Yes, but I think what you really want is a domestic." He does more of the house cleaning than I do.*
David 40   *We've had such a commitment all along, we've been so close.*
David 45   *We both are HIV positive. We both are healthy but our immune system is beginning to decrease so we're both making a commitment that whoever gets sick first, the other one will be taken care of. That made a major change in how we view our relationship. It is probably a shorter term relationship.*
David 40   *One thing about gay relationships that is unique, is it's a real commitment. You're not forced into it because you have a piece of paper or children you're protecting from reality. You keep pledging yourself and it keeps working. I see so many straights locked in because they have a piece of paper. We've committed ourselves for so long without that.*

---❤---

Anita 35   *Just love and friendship and respect.*

---❤---

Bert 45   *We promised to cherish and support each other in our hopes and dreams. We promised to share our lives, care for each other's health, and to create a warm and comfortable home. We said, "I am your partner in life. Receive this ring as a reminder of my promise to you." Those were our wedding vows.*

---❤---

Gwen 26   *A lot of it hasn't been in a spoken formal way. I know that I can trust Deena and she'll take care of me if anything happens to me.*

---❤---

Eric 29   *To love him in sickness and in health and to be faithful to him.*

Steven 45   *A depth of commitment that is basic enough, that whatever conflict there is, we'll put in the time and the honesty to work it out. I'm HIV positive, myself, and that in itself is a source of commitment for both of us. We both have wills and durable power of attorney for medical care. We're looking into replacing our will with a living trust.*

<hr>

David 40   *This is my lover and my life partner and my promise is just to be there always for him.*

Hugh 46   *I promised to myself and David to be with each other and listen and be willing to invest the energy needed to build the relationship. It's a growing thing, and like anything live and growing it needs care and without that care and nourishment that thing becomes a dry stick and is dead.*

David   *I've committed to always doing the laundry and Hugh's committed to feeding me...but, it's still about this dusting.*

<hr>

Wade 34   *That I love Brent and will love him and that I'm there when he needs me. The bottom line is, that I promised him that I care for him and that I will be there.*

Brent 38   *I've made a commitment to share my life with Wade and to be his companion. We met each other when both of us were very new to being gay. We were still students. We don't really know any other life. We were in school when we met. We went from being high-schoolers into college into a relationship. We didn't have any other relationship.*

<hr>

Lauren 29   *A lifetime, long before Domestic Partners came up. That was clear to us after the first year.*

<hr>

Richard 28   *That we would always try to work out any problems that came up and talk them out and not let anger take the best and walk away from the situation.*

Ken 45   *Probably, the same things that everybody promises each other, to take care of and respect the other person and love the other person in the relationship.*

<hr>

Simone 52   *To love, nurture, support, and cherish. We promised if ever we had trouble communicating, that we would seek counselling.*

<hr>

Steve 35   *We wrote our own vows, we wrote the whole ceremony.*

Phillip 27 *To stand by each other regardless what life brings...good times and bad times, happy times and sad times.*

Steve *To encourage each other's individual growth through our own individual lives, but at the same time build a life together.*

Phillip *The part of our wedding ceremony where we said our vows together, were said over an open flame. It's a Buddhist tradition, I think, that if two people say a promise over an open flame it seals it forever. We had an open flame between us and we held hands and said these vows together in front of this packed church with all our friends and family. It was very special.*

Rachel 30 *We made a promise to be together as long as we both shall live. We have no expectations that this relationship is going to end short of one or the other of us dying. We have made a promise to each other to have a monogamous relationship and to raise a child together.*

Lynn 38 *Recently, we cleaned up paper work in terms of wills and durable powers of attorney and for health care and legal decisions. We are each other's primary beneficiary and each other's person who should make health care decisions and what not.*

Jackie 40 *We haven't taken our respect, caring, and love for one another and defined it in a ritualistic way of putting into words to each other. I know that there is a definite acknowledgment and sense of longevity and total partnership in terms of who we choose to spend the rest of our lives with, which is each other. We're planning retirement.*

Larry 45 *To be the best possible friend and the best possible lover I can be to Wood. That means honesty. I want to be as honest as I can be about my feelings about him and about us. To communicate honestly and clearly and to be as intimate as I could possibly be with him. I would try to share as much as I can physically and emotionally and mentally and psychologically. I pledged to him to remain a best friend for myself, to have solitude, to have independence, to not think that Wood has to provide my every need. I have some needs he can't provide and to be honest about that and to continue to be a whole person not a half a person. I want our relationship to be whatever it is we want it to be. We don't have to copy heterosexuals. We have the freedom, the wit and the intelligence and the commitment to make our relationship work for us no matter what that means, even if it's not traditional.*

Wood 45 *To love Larry as completely as I could, no matter what may* *come. To confront directly and openly any conflict that happens to us. To respect his privacy, to support, honor, and love him the rest of my life.*

Kevin 37   *I think we take each other for granted. Dan will always be a part of my life and he will help provide for our family as I do.*
Dan 37   *I really do trust Kevin and I trust myself.*

Chuck 38   *We promised an unassailable, unimpeachable, emotional bond. Nothing gets in the way of our emotional commitment to one another.*

Annette 32   *To be true to the commitment and be monogamous to the relationship. That our love will endure and persevere through the years.*
Sandy 35   *We promised to be honest and to check in with each other on a daily basis and that once you started a sentence, you had to finish it. To some people, that doesn't make much sense, but when you're in the heat of a discussion or if you're trying to explain something, sometimes you might think, "How do I say this so that the other person will accept it?" instead of, "How do I say it to get my emotions out?" So, we both say what we need to say and we finish our sentences. If we don't, the other person calls us on it. It's been one of the greatest things we have done.*

Dick 60   *We've promised to be sexually monogamous and to stay with our relationship for affection.*
Otto 60   *To love and care for each other. We didn't start out saying we're going to be together for thirty years. As a matter of fact, it's been a surprise.*

Alice 40   *To hang in there, no matter what. We promised if we ever have a fight that we never go to bed angry. We've committed to honesty.*

James 29   *That we would be together as long as we thought it was a good idea.*

Katherine 40   *To love each other through sickness and in health, to love and honor each other forever, forsaking all others.*

Coni 39   *We intend to be together for as long as we live. We have a monogamous relationship.*

Jane 49   *We are totally committed to each other. The trust base is so important.*

Coni   *We know that we're soul mates. I happened, in this lifetime, to find the one. What's most important is not to say to one another that we are going to be together forever and ever, but to choose it everyday, to live in the moment. That's what builds the strongest possible relationship.*

———————❤———————

Susan 33   *Basically, unconditional love.*

Marty 32   *Friendship, companionship and to be supportive of each other in whatever endeavors we choose to take on.*

Susan   *I promised, not only to always be there for her, no matter what, but to be honest and trusting. I've learned through the years, that without those things, you don't really have a relationship.*

What would terminate your relationship?

Anita 35   *Probably infidelity.*
Lori 28   *Any time we argue or fight or anything, I just think about the day we got married and that was the greatest day in my entire life. When you say, love at first sight, I really know that. For me, the minute I saw her that was it for me.*

Jack 60   *Death.*

Gwen 26   *Either one of us growing very much apart from the other or a really cataclysmic breach of trust.*
Deena 23   *Since we're monogamous, it would probably be some affair, because both of us are incredibly jealous.*

Tony 39   *If we didn't love each other anymore.*

Eric 29   *Death of one of us.*

David 40   *If one of us died.*

Brent 38   *I've never thought about that. We've been through a lot together.*

Kit 39   *Infidelity would be a real problem or a major felony. Either of those is a real serious issue, but we might work it out. My approach to that is, I don't want to set any ultimatums and draw any real hard and fast lines and say if you do that, that's it, forget it, it's over with. I don't need to set out challenges like that.*

Jane 29   *If one of us got terminated.*
Lauren 29   *The only thing we ever think of is power of attorneys because...God forbid, if anything would happen to one of us. That's the terms of which we think of in our relationship. Thinking of the future is...oh my God, we have to protect each other, not what do I do to make sure that I get this when this relationship is over...what do I do to make sure some money is put away for me. Everything's joint. In our first year, we had joint checking accounts.*

Brad 30   *Death or a decision from us to end the relationship and* *maybe not death. Nothing external could end it.*

———————❤———————

Richard 28   *A total breakdown in communications. I haven't really thought in those terms.*
Wally 37   *A hidden affair, outside the relationship, that had not been discussed.*

———————❤———————

Ken 45   *Death is all I can think about. I don't see anything else.*
Jay 41   *Why think about it? When you meet somebody and say, "Well, when I break up with him..." Why think of negative things?*

———————❤———————

Anne 38   *I don't think anything would terminate our relationship. I think she could even be unfaithful. We're strongly monogamous, and we could work through it. Maybe, if either one of us became so self-destructive in some way.*

———————❤———————

Phillip 27   *We've already been through so much together. I can't think of anything.*
Steve 35   *Dishonesty. The day we got back from our honeymoon, we found out that Phillip had a malignancy. Dealing with cancer has really put us through our paces.*

———————❤———————

Lynn 38   *Some horrendous betrayal of trust.*
Jackie 40   *But, based on how well we know each other, the likelihood of something like that happening is not great enough to consider it as an option. That's why I say death is the only thing.*

———————❤———————

Adria-Ann 43   *At this point it feels so healthy and good that it's hard to say. Will our age difference be more important in the future?*

———————❤———————

Larry 45   *If Wood's values changed significantly. It's very important that his values are values of freedom and support for ending racism and sexism and homophobia. If he stopped respecting my need for privacy, or if he smoked, or hit me.*

———————❤———————

Jeff 38   *It would never happen. We're umbilically and telepathically linked. Most people that are together so long, think less about it. The people I always meet, who say they never can have a relationship, are those people who already have predefined ideas about what relationships are and they can't have those things. When something does come along,*

because it doesn't meet that check list they have, then it never happens. We don't need those predefined things, because we know exactly what it is we need and want that makes us work and happy. All of that's right here and we don't need to go anywhere to find it. What is, is.
Steve 37 *Nothing. It's hard for me to imagine. In former relationships, it was easier to image things like that. With this one, it's different.*

❤

Sandy 35 *For me, it would be death.*
Annette 32 *The relationship would be in serious trouble if there were a third person. I'm not sure it would end it, but it would be a very serious moment.*

❤

Dick 60 *Death.*

❤

Alice 40 *A real serious lack of communication. We'd have to be on the skids for a long time and finally realize it's not working any more. I'm in here for the long haul.*

❤

John 33 *The only thing that would, would be death.*
James 29 *I think so, too. We're really the best of friends. Even if we weren't lovers any more, we would still be best friends and live together.*

❤

Katherine 40 *I don't think it's an option.*

❤

Susan 33 *The one thing that would not immediately terminate it, but would cause the greatest problem, would be extra-marital relations.*
Marty 32 *Death. I'm going to spend my life with this woman. We want to have a child, probably in the next year or so.*

How would you like to see the law?

Gael 35 *Everything, I want everything. I want tax benefits, I want it just to be a given that if Denise is sick or in the hospital, I'm consulted, that I am recognized as her partner. I know and understand her desires and her will. I want our income to be considered jointly for anything we would do that would cause indebtedness, a house or whatever.*

Denise 30 *If Gael got sick and she was married to a man, they would call her husband and say, "What should we do?" We have a living will and powers of attorney. The family could still overrule. If my family was rotten and obstinate, they could still fight and if I had a fortune they could still try to take the fortune away from her. It's been done to gay people.*

Gael *Denise is diabetic. I have this incredible health insurance plan at my firm. It would be great if I could have her on it and I can't. There's all these kind of discounts that you can pass on to family members. I belong to a credit union and I was thrilled to find out that they let me define family, but I had expected a fight.*

---❤---

John 35 *I would like to see the wording stronger and include more, because right now we don't have any protection in terms of discrimination against us. I am ready for more of an acceptance in society than we're currently given.*

Richard 37 *I would like to see Domestic Partners have all the same benefits and rights as marriage and not have to call it anything different. We would like to really be married. We'd like to adopt if we chose to, or file joint income tax, or have health insurance. It doesn't seem like that much to ask for. We're giving the same or more as any other family or couple. We're part of our community. We vote. We may do volunteer work to enrich our community.*

John *We're paying taxes.*

---❤---

Lori 28 *That it's legal and binding and we do have some rights. The right to designate the person you want. Anita has a liver dysfunction and I do all the phoning and dealing with the bills and speaking with the doctors. No one recognizes me and it really upsets me. Well, her doctor does now and that's really nice. I'm there, I care, I go to all the doctor's appointments.*

Anita 35 *If it could just go to the next step where we could get married in the State and be a couple and have community property. Whenever you have to sign anything, like at school, I could check off married. I want to* *be treated just like every other married person.*

Lori   *For our vacation, I got an oil company credit card. I put her down for a second one and they both came under my name. I called them and said I want the second one with her name on it and the bill comes to me. We did it on the phone, went over it, they read it back and they still sent the second one with my name on it.*

Q   Why didn't you say this is my sister, my married sister?
Anita   *But we don't want to have to do that.*

Lori   *I came from a really strict background, just as normal as can be, very Brady Bunch. I'm extremely open-minded and I'm very proud of where I'm at right now. I don't want to have to lie or hide.*

------------------❤------------------

Bert 45   *I'd like to have the same benefits that any married people have, no more and no less. If it was to our advantage to file joint income tax or to be on each other's health insurance, we should have that. I don't care so much about the legality of being married. It's nice to have our Domestic Partnership on the wall and I look at it all the time. It's an acknowledgment from the City. The marriage ceremony we did, means a lot more because it's something we created for ourselves. The only reason I would really like to be married in the eyes of the law, is for the benefits. I want the perks that married people get. We're doing all the rest.*

------------------❤------------------

Gwen 26   *I would like to be able to be on each other's insurance policies. If Deena went into the hospital and couldn't speak for her own rights, I would like it to be legally acknowledged that we do have a relationship and I would be allowed to visit her and help take care of her. Generally, it's the next of kin that speaks for them, unless they're married. You can get that by power of attorney and you can get a lot of the other rights, as far as what would happen if one of us dies, by going through and making out complicated wills and legal papers.*

If you're gay and you want to get all those things through the legal process, you have to pay a pretty good chunk of money to do it and you have to keep a lawyer employed for several years because the law changes minutely every year.

I would hope that in the future we will be able to keep the Domestic Partnership that we have now as it's written and build on it and have it powerful enough to implement those things and have it be recognized by corporations that you work for so you can get bereavement.

------------------❤------------------

Tony 39   *To be on a par with heterosexual marriage with the legal privileges that they have. Marriage would not corrupt our relationship.*

There aren't these role playing models that we would have to fit into if we were a straight couple getting married. Society has, in general, expectations of what the husband is and what the wife is and who cares for the house, etc. It wouldn't be true in our case; we've made our own rules for the last fifteen years.

❤

David 40 *To have the same kind of rights that a regular married couple would have. This is a separate and unequal status.*

Hugh 46 *I think we should get married and I've proposed and we would if we could.*

❤

Brent 38 *Ideally, I think marriage should not recognize gender.*

Wade 34 *There is a separate set of laws, that will someday be impacted by all of this, which is...do I have the right, working for Safeway, to say that Brent is on my health plan?*

Brent *Why you want to have marriage between the two of us, is that society will recognize us as being just as valid as a male/female marrying. We contribute to society just as much as any other couple. I think it's a long ways away.*

❤

Helene 39 *I would like to see it give the same kind of legal rights that heterosexual couples currently have in terms of the benefits with the tax laws, with being able to get your partner on your insurance, any kind of benefits you get when your partner dies, and all kinds of little things that are written into the law.*

If I have a car and I want to get Kit's name on that title, I can do that without paying the sales tax, if the name going on there is either my spouse, parent, or sibling. If it's not a person that's legally related to me, they say I've got to pay the tax. If I was married to a man and I went in there and said, "I want to add my husband to this," they would say, "Fine."

Kit 39 *Most of those practical things that kick in for heterosexual couples that get married are benefits for making things cheaper. Change the marriage laws to have any two persons marry.*

Legal marriage is not a guarantee of anything. What it does is give a little more legitimacy to society at large to the commitment the couple has made to each other. You get a little more respect, most of the time, from people around you.

If a legally married couple talks about splitting up and getting a divorce, there are more tangible things they have to do in order to make that happen. Friends and family tend to say, "Come on, give it another chance." There's more support for staying together. Without that kind of legal sanction to the relationship, it's a lot easier to get out of in most cases, and quicker because there isn't the legal stuff to hassle with. The fact that marriage isn't enjoying a lot of success doesn't mean that it shouldn't be an option for those people that want to have it. To take that argument further would mean, because it's not working for some people then nobody should have the option of being married.

Helene   *If it were to be accepted, the relationship could be taken for granted as much as I think roles are assumed and relationships taken for granted in a lot of heterosexual marriages. We might have the same kind of troubles. What I see right now is, we have to work so hard at just surviving this relationship. We have a much more intentional relationship than a lot of the straight people I know.*

———————————❤———————————

Jane 29   *I prefer that the Domestic Partnership law didn't exist and we could get married if we wanted to.*

Lauren 29   *I'd like to have Jane covered on my benefits, to take advantage of the tax breaks, and not to have to go through all the hassle of getting a power of attorney and a will and just be automatically protected just as a marriage would protect it.*

Jane   *You can only get married when you're straight and straight relationships, by their nature, have these predetermined roles and these predetermined expectations. They're not known to foster any kind of complete independence. No matter how open-minded either one of the participants is, you're still bound by all the centuries of what's conventional in a straight relationship.*

———————————❤———————————

Brad 30   *That the current laws would include non-traditional relationships, and that they not be restricted to just the traditional marriage relationships. Anyone who decides that they love each other and want to spend the time and effort and pain to make that commitment stick should be recognized. Existing laws could be altered to remove the restriction for opposite sex.*

———————————❤———————————

Richard 28   *The same as a legal marriage for a heterosexual couple. They should remove the words man and woman and put in two people.*

Wally 37   *I would like to see it change on a national level, mandated by the Supreme Court as equal rights for same sex couples. And I would like it to extend so that every company in the United States is required to give health insurance, death benefits, and visitation rights, and we can file taxes together.*

Richard   *Marriage tends to falter a lot. Usually one person tends to see that as the ultimate commitment and once they've made that they're not happy with it. Once they're in a marriage, they're safe. It loses the edge that you've got to keep things going good or else. It tends to kill some of the excitement.*

♥

Ken 45   *The same rights and privileges as a married couple. I don't think a San Francisco ordinance would accomplish that. The laws don't need to be gender specific.*

♥

Anne 38   *I would rewrite State law to go back to the definition of a marriage. I would say a legal marriage is between two people.*
Simone 52   *It's too idealistic. I would like to have a society where you didn't need a law. Why do we need a law for Anne and I to be permitted to love each other? Do you need a law that says that you have to love a man? Why do I need a law to love a woman? I want to be able to go with Anne and no one think anything about it. I want to be able to kiss her goodbye right in the middle of Main St. if she goes off on the bus and I go off on my stuff for the day. You have that freedom to kiss someone in the middle of Kansas and go off to your job and he can go off to his job.*
   Anne   *If we had legal sanctions, would 50% of our relationships fall apart in the same way that 50% of the heterosexual relationships fall apart? We could. Relationships take a lot of work and I don't think that it has anything to do with being straight, gay, or whatever. Those of us who registered for Domestic Partnership are that much more committed than our fellow gays and lesbians who are in relationships.*

♥

Phillip 27   *There wouldn't be Domestic Partnership, there would simply be marriage and anyone can get married, a man and a woman, or two men and two women. All the contractual things that come with marriage, like rights of inheritance and all that, applies equally to everyone. Steve and I have wills and powers of attorney. We've taken the legal steps we had to take. Heterosexuals don't have to do these extra legal steps. If they change the law tomorrow and same sex couples could go down and get married, we would do it for the tax benefits if nothing else. It infuriates me that we can't file a joint return.*

♥

Rachel 30   *I have some problems with the traditional institution of marriage in our culture. That's one of the criticisms of Domestic Partnership, that we're just going out there and trying to ape heterosexual* *marriage. I would like to see contracts or agreements between people for different specific purposes, such as rearing a child or a loving relationship that's going to be mutually supportive. I don't think that it has to be limited to two people. Three people might decide that they want to rear a child and live together and have legal and economic recognition for the fact that they're a household unit of three adults equally participating.*

Joan 45   *They may or may not be in a sexual relationship.*

Rachel   *That might be the crux of it. I have real problems with the need to create a legal structure for legitimate and illegitimate sexual relations. It's absolutely outrageous that we still have people being prosecuted for adultery in the country. I have no objection to people of whatever religion having whatever kinds of relations their religion calls for, but I feel that should be outside the legal realm.*

Lynn 38   *I want the same benefits as a married couple so that we don't end up having to lie on various applications and things in order to take advantage of the spousal bundle discount. One or the other of us uses a first initial. That irritates the hell out of me.*

Jackie 40   *We both have Ph.D.'s, so we put Dr. down. Of course, it's got to be a man.*

Adria-Ann 43   *I work in immigration law and see a lot of gay couples come to me, one of them being a foreigner. There's absolutely no way that the partner can confer citizenship on his or her partner. That causes tremendous hardship and anxiety and impossible living situations on people who are in love as a couple.*

Wood 45   *Everyone could get married and be treated equally in our society if they were married or single, regardless of sexuality or gender, and groups of people could get married.*

Steve 30   *We would be given the tax benefits nationally and health benefits.*

Ken 32   *I want my relationship accepted as equally as a married couple.*

Steve   *Heterosexual men and women have these preconceived roles that, conscious or unconscious, they want their partner to slip into if they get married. There are no set roles or rules for our kind of relationships, because there are no role models.*

Ken   *There have been role models set up all through history for* *male/female couples as to how you play the game of being married. The man goes out and supports the family and the wife stays and cooks and that's what happens when you get married. It's like the 50's traditional family. Women have been trying since the 60's to break out of that.*

Steve *Men and women have to fight to get out of those roles. I think it's neat that we don't have that.*

Ken *If they let us get married, we would be a lot happier in the fact that now, we're finally accepted as normal human beings.*

---❤---

Dan 37 *Marriage would be quite different than for straight people, because it would simply be an option for gay and lesbian people. Perhaps, you would get only those couples who really and truly wanted to be married, for whatever reason, as opposed to in the straight community where there's still this social push, expectation, and norm to be married. Perhaps that has more to do with divorce rates than marriage per se as an option for people who want to live together.*

In the gay community, the people who are against marriage won't get married. There's nobody pushing them to get married and wondering why didn't you get married, why aren't you married, what's wrong with you.

The same is true with gay and lesbian parenting. Those people who really and truly want to raise kids are seeking out how to get kids. There are no accidental kids. It's not as easy as being in a straight relationship. Literally, one morning you can wake up and say, "Honey guess what, I skipped my period, I think I'm going to go see the doctor." "...but...but...but...you said you were on the pill."

Gay people have a choice to be a parent. There's not an expectation to get married and hear, "Boy, you've been married for three years and still don't have a kid, what's wrong, what's happening, something's wrong in the bedroom." In a gay or lesbian relationship, this is not the case. There's not this social pressure to be married, to have kids. Forbidding us the option is the crime. That's discrimination. The great social pressure on the straight community to be married and to be parents. It is terrible for the kids who get brought into the world when maybe they're not wanted, but somehow it's expected for whatever the reason.

Q Would marriage change your relationship?

Dan *It would make life easier. Just in terms of having a daughter. We could get family health insurance, in terms of tax purposes, auto insurance, etc.*

Kevin 37 *...and basic concerns that if something happens to one of us, who has Sarah...the ease of adopting a child as a couple versus two individuals.*

Dan   *I would like to be similar to a heterosexual couple, because then if they still were against me, we would get closer to the real issues. Then we would start talking about homophobia. It has nothing to do with the sanctity of marriage and family life. Those would all be out the window and we would discuss the real issues of why people are so adamantly against us.*

Kevin   *It would be a nice way to publicly affirm what we hope to do with our lives. Whether you have a piece of paper that states you're married or whether you have a Domestic Partnership piece of paper or whether you have none of that, there's always the possibility it's not going to work out.*

———————————♥———————————

Otto 60   *I'd like to see homosexuals treated the same way as any other heterosexual couple would be treated under the law. Under the religious aspect, I don't believe a homosexual relationship need be acknowledged by the church. This is a thing that every couple has to decide for themselves, whether or not they need some acknowledgement of their relationship.*

Dick 60   *I think it's an equal protection issue.*

———————————♥———————————

Ben 32   *Marriage, actually. There are two things that people oppose, gay marriage and gays serving in the military. Those are two virtues that are held very highly by the straight people. We're just asking for the same thing.*

Todd 27   *A lot of people within the gay community reject marriage along the heterosexual line as being archaic and dated. The 50's had a model of monogamy between two people for the rest of their lives. People in the 90's are a lot more aware that sometimes things are not forever and things aren't always between two people.*

Ben   *In some circles in the homosexual community, you find people who don't participate in Domestic Partnership because they feel that it's not enough. They want to see alternative marriages within the same sex and also between more than one person, or two people in the group.*

———————————♥———————————

Richard 30   *I'd like to get tax breaks. There should be same sex marriages allowing every benefit that a man and a woman who get married can have.*

Chris 33   *What we really need is to make everybody the same in this country. The marriage laws, from the divorces I've seen, apparently don't work as well as they could in terms of protecting everone's legal rights.*

What I interpret the United States Constitution to mean, when they say all men are created equal, is that we all should have the same thing, regardless of what it is. If there are problems with the marriage laws as they exist for the heterosexuals that are getting married, then we should all have to deal with them rather than produce some seperate laws for homosexuals. I would apply the marriage laws to everyone.

❤

Jane 49   *People should have access and benefits. The same kind of rights for everyone.*

Coni 39   *We would have to come up with a way to document being partnered, whether or not we have a civil ceremony like people do to get married. Many of us are not in favor of just simply trying to go after the marriage model, because it has its roots in domination. Marriage came about because women were property of the man. They were handed over from their father directly to the husband.*

Jane   *The first romantic services that were done in churches were done around gay people. From the third to the fourteenth century they were doing gay and lesbian marriages. The other ones were property things.*

Coni   *Marriage as a model does not look good to us. That model is not mutuality. We should have as many rights as any heterosexual couple would have being a couple. Our unions should be legal and from that everything else would follow.*

Jane   *Or, you just do Domestic Partnership for everyone. Then you have a balance of mutuality.*

Coni   *That doesn't address the children. I'm not sure the rights of children would be fully protected.*

❤

Marty 32   *I'd like to see gay and lesbian marriages legalized and that people really have to take responsibility for each other.*

Susan 33   *I wouldn't expect it to be different than marriage, financial responsibility and all.*

Tell me about your family and friends.

Denise 30   *Friends reacted positively, if they reacted at all. People knew we had worked on the campaign and the election before when it didn't pass. We wrote letters to almost everybody we knew, people we worked with and friends, telling them how important this was to us, what it meant to us, and asking them to go out and vote for it. People knew it was something we wanted. Some people sent us cards and some people called.*

Gael 35   *One friend sent us Tupperware. I think my mother accepts our relationship a little better. She accepted it fine before, but her acceptance seems to have gotten a little deeper.*

Denise   *I have two brothers. One has been great. He used to be rednecky. My other brother sent us a card. Now he asks about Gael. Instead of saying, "How are you doing?" he now purposely asks, "How is she doing?" and, "What are you guys up to?" In that way, it's made her more real.*

Gael   *My mother doesn't talk about me to her friends or the other parts of the family. I went down recently to visit her and her sister and for that day Denise did not exist.*

Denise   *There was a lot of support when we sent out our announcements. It's wonderful to have that support. When people get married, they have parties and showers.*

John 35   *Within the eight years, we've been very open and out with friends, family, and employers. It wasn't a matter of having the important people recognize us as a couple, because that had already happened.*

Richard 37   *Legally we had taken steps to insure that our relationship would be recognized. We have powers of attorney and we own our home together. We have all those things that legally are more binding than Domestic Partnership.*

Lori 28   *We've always been recognized as a couple by our friends.*

Anita 35   *My family is supportive, but Lori's is not. They know we have done this.*

Lori   *Through word of mouth, they found out. They're just very closed-minded individuals.*

Anita   *But her grandmother's great, she accepts me. She's really terrific.*

Jack 60   *Never one day in our lives have we had even the slightest* *prejudice among our friends and our families. Now our second generation relatives, their in-laws, are suspicious of us because of ACT UP and men walking around with their ass hanging out and women riding around with their teats showing in the Gay Parade. There's not the same amount of warmth and acceptance among the second and third generations as there used to be.*

Gwynn 28   *My family is not accepting at all. They are Fundamentalist Christians.*

Bert 45   *My family has been supportive for many years. They have been unbelievingly accepting of Gwynn, they just love him to death. They participated in our wedding.*

Gwen 26   *My dad was real happy. My mom kind of freaked out. We're slowly sliding my parents into the idea of a Holy Union. They don't have any problem with me being a lesbian but they want to make sure that their little girl is careful and doesn't rush into things. My mom loves Deena to bits, but when I told her about this she said, "We'll, it's a marriage, are you sure you want to do this? It's a big step." I told her I considered Domestic Partnership a definite step, but to me it's not the same thing. The Holy Union will be a marriage. This is like a formalized engagement.*

Deena 23   *I was out at work years ago and they've conveniently forgotten everything I told them, so I didn't tell them at work. My family and I don't really speak very much.*

The closest person to me is my grandmother and she knows but she won't allow me to tell her that I'm a lesbian. Once she said ,"There's a lot of things that I know about you that you don't think I know, but I want you to know that I know...just don't tell me and we'll be fine." She still loves me anyway. Gwen and I are monogamous. We're relatively safe people. We don't do drugs, we don't go out and have illicit affairs with people.

Eric 29   *My family is accepting for the most part.*

Steve 45   *My father died before I came out. My mother has essentially looked the other way, never accepting me as a gay man. It is something I have put behind me in my daily life. I wish it were otherwise, but it's not. I write her long letters and tell her about the wonderful things that are going on in our lives. I get these letters back that talk about the weather and never mention my partner. She is welcome to visit anytime she wants. I would send her airfare. I told her I will come and visit anytime if she will invite me and my partner.*

———————❤———————

Brent 38   *Family goes through an evolution, too. It doesn't happen right away. It takes time for them to develop trust of the other partner. They go through a coming out just like we do.*

Wade 34   *For gay people, part of the process of coming to grips with the fact that you're gay is that you have to acknowledge it exists. You deal with all the internal homophobia you may have from society and then you build out of that. You finally come to accept who you are and where you are. I think the very same process happens with your parents. You tell them and it's like, "No I don't like that." then, "No, this is really real, it really does exist, they are really that way, I still don't like it but..." and then eventually it's, "Well, what difference does it make?"*

Brent   *My parents have evolved from actively hiding it from everybody to actively telling everybody. My mother is very proud of it, she likes to tell people.*

Wade   *One of the things that was very nice about the first day for Domestic Partnership was that it was Valentine's Day and it was Chinese New Year's Eve.*

Brent   *For my family, New Year's Eve evening is a very important family occasion. You all go home to your family and have a festive dinner. We went straight from the Domestic Partnership ceremony to my parents' home with the document in hand. My parents were very happy. Symbolically, it was very important to my parents that there was a binding of this relationship and an acknowledgment from some higher authority that this is real. My mother bought china for all of her sons for their weddings, intending to give them to them as they got married. She gave me a set of china.*

Wade   *We had this relationship, but it wasn't until we did the Domestic Partnership that it was official, and thereby now the wedding gift was appropriate.*

Brent   *Another thing Chinese tend to do at weddings is give a lot of jewelry. My mother's been giving us a lot of jewelry lately.*

Wade   *One of the first things his family mentioned was, "When are we going to have the wedding banquet?" In the Chinese culture, the wedding banquet is as important as the wedding. We waited for my mom to come out for the banquet.*

———————❤———————

Kit 39   *Parts of our families were willing to be present at our wedding. My gay brother was very supportive. He died two years ago.*

Helene 39   *My parents were not willing to be there. Kit's parents were*

*not very thrilled about being there but were appropriate and polite.
Relations between Kit's parents and me, and us as a couple, have greatly
improved in the last few years.*

---♥---

Jane 29   *My family doesn't know.*

Lauren 29   *I came out to my family about two or three years ago. As of
this year, probably because of Domestic Partnership, I'm exhibiting how
confident I am. I don't care who knows, pretty much. I'm not going to
blatantly put it on my back, but Jane's with me for life and I think that
shows when I'm talking to my parents. My parents know I'm very serious
about this. They weren't accepting in the beginning at all. Now they're
seeing that I'm very happy, I'm competent, I'm independent, and healthy.
They realize Jane is good for me and I'm good for Jane, so they are
accepting now. They say, "How's Jane? Send Jane my love." Just to hear
that over the phone is wonderful.*

Q   What caused their acceptance?

Lauren   *I think, probably my attitude had a lot to do with it, not fearing
it and skirting around the issue. I was really nervous to my family. Years
ago in my first gay relationship I was caught and sent to a psychiatrist. I
was going to be kicked out of the house. They took me out of school and
put me in another school where there were no lesbians. I was nineteen.
According to my family, I was "cured." Then, I started bringing Jane
around and my family started to freak. They wanted nothing to do with
Jane. They didn't want to know her name; they didn't want her in the
house; they didn't want her coming by. Then I moved to San Francisco
with Jane and now they're realizing I'm not going to grow out of it, that
I'm healthy, and everything's fine.*

Jane   *I always felt like Marlon Brando, driving up to pick her up at her
parents' house. They were looking out the windows, wishing I would
disappear. They finally realized that there's nothing that their dreamed for
son-in-law had that I didn't have. I went to the school they liked, I have a
good job, and I'm responsible. They were afraid that this radical lesbian
would carry her off into the woods or something like that.*

---♥---

Joan 24   *My mother is still working through accepting having a gay
daughter. All her life, she worked with gay people and accepted gay
people. She's had gay friends, she had a gay boss for years and years, a
gay piano teacher, and she didn't care. But when she found out her own
daughter was gay, it was very hard for her to work through. She's still
working through it and I'm still working through being comfortable with*

her. *If you're a parent, you set up certain expectations for a child and one of those isn't being gay.*

We went through a bad time in high school with it. The first woman I went out with was very unstable and that contributed a lot to my mother's fear and dislike of the situation. I went away to college and there was a long period where we just didn't talk about it. Now that she's seen me in a stable relationship and has met Louise, little by little things are getting better.

Louise 28   *My mother met Joan before she knew that she was my lover and liked her a lot. Then, she found out she was my lover and didn't like that at all. She's been very accepting of Joan and asks about her, but underneath it all, she thinks it's the worst thing that could have happened to her daughter that she had so much hope for. She wanted me to be the lovely socialite wife of a nice, young businessman. Her pain in thinking that she doesn't have a nice, normal, married daughter, is going to lessen in time I hope.*

———————❤———————

Brad 30   *Our families both accept us as a non-traditional family.*

Carl 46   *My mom grew up in a traditional WASP environment and held real traditional views. I think I've been a real education for her. One of the lessons she learned is that love, commitment, trust, and a sense of belonging, don't really depend on your sex or your sexual orientation. When she saw how I was with people and how the people she met through me were, she realized a lot of the things that she had been taught as a child to believe as true, weren't true.*

———————❤———————

Richard 28   *They are accepting of our relationship with each other. They weren't real thrilled with us being in the newspaper. They're happy to see I have someone to be happy with and settle down with.*

Wally 37   *My mother has learned to accept it. She still says that I'd make a great father and it was unfortunate that I wasn't comfortable with the idea of having a wife and some kids. One time she said "When are you going to settle down?" I knew what she was getting at, "When are you going to stop playing around with all these gay boys and get a wife and have some kids?" I said "Mom, when I find the right man."*

———————❤———————

Jay 41   *When we became Domestic Partners, my sister said, "Am I supposed to send a wedding present or something?"*

———————❤———————

Simone 52   *My father is supportive, he always was. He is much more*

*worldly than my mother ever was. He may not be educated and he is also
an Italian immigrant, but the man reads three newspapers everyday from
cover to cover. He's been very in tune to gay and lesbian articles.*

Anne 38 *A lot of people think their children should be extensions of
themselves. They think their children should be what they think their
children should be, not what their children are.*

Simone *When my older girls date someone, or even to a friend, they
have to come out. Sooner or later, they have to say, "My mother's a
lesbian." My oldest said, "It's great, it's a wonderful barometer. I tell them
my mother's a lesbian. If they can't accept it, they're assholes and I don't
put any more energy into the relationship."*

———————————❤———————————

Phillip 27 *My brother is the only one that I have any kind of a
relationship with. That's not just because I'm gay. It encompassed a lot of
other things. Being gay was just the icing on the cake.*

Q Does that hurt you?

Phillip *It used to. For a long time, I wished things were different. As I
got older, I just accepted it. My ideal fantasy would be different, but this is
just the way things are. I have lots of wonderful people in my life that I
love and love me back. I have created my own family and that's what I'm
happy with.*

———————————❤———————————

Lynn 38 *We're both out to our families. Mine is tolerant to varying
degrees. They accept that I have chosen a life-style that they're glad
nobody else in the family has chosen. Acceptance, I think, is too
optimistic of a word. They speak to me and we have a loving relationship
on some level, but they don't understand Jackie and me.*

Jackie 40 *My parents are genuinely fond of Lynn and very accepting of
our relationship. I'm their daughter and they love me and they're glad that
there's this nice solid Mid-Western woman who's good to me. Certainly,
they would rather I be heterosexual. They don't really understand what it
is to be lesbian or gay and everything that goes into that.*

Q What do you think would make them have more understanding?

Lynn *Thirty years in California, out of the Mid-West.*

Jackie *There's a distance. There's a bother of sorts there. Part of it is
that we're all involved, regardless of our sexual orientation, with the
growing up process, and also recognizing that Jackie's my family. Had
there been an easier time and easier process of relationship development
in our society than what I've experienced in my life, maybe it wouldn't be
as bothersome as it is. Maybe, had I gone through some things that other*

people go through, the rituals of marriage, etc., that are built in for heterosexuals, I would have confronted some of these things in a different way earlier. It's been through my relationship with Jackie that I really began to realize that Jackie is my family. Yes, I love these people, but they're not really my family in the sense in which a woman married with children would think.

Q   How did your friends feel?

Jackie   *It pointed out to them how nice it is that they have the options they have. There was an acknowledgment from them about how nice it was that we had this token gesture that you were allowed to do. It pointed out to them that we don't get medical benefits, we don't get this and that and we don't have parties, and we don't have a wedding ceremony. When we go to our straight friends' weddings we say jokingly, "Hey, when are they going to buy us a wedding present?"*

Kris 26   *My parents are divorced, so I think we consider our family to be my mother and her mother. My mother has loved Adria-Ann from the beginning. She was upset at first when I came out, denying the reality of it. She became more accepting of it, ultimately because she values her relationship with me too much to sacrifice it over my sexuality. She would rather get over it and make sure we're close than to hold that against me.*

Adria-Ann 43   *When I first came out my mother cried, was very upset, and told me she didn't want me to bring any of my "friends" around.*

Wood 45   *My family's not accepting at all. My younger sister is accepting, but my older sister is not, and neither of their husbands can accept us at all. My father has a very hard time with it. He's a Fundamentalist Christian. He hasn't disowned me, but he thinks our relationship is an abomination. It's hurt for years. It's really a horribly painful thing to go through. I've known since I was seven that I was gay. You get used to it and learn to deal with it and cope. I must say, since I've been with Larry, it's been such a relief to be around his family. It's such a joy for me to go and play cards with his sister and brother-in-law. His mother will be there and I'm just like part of the family. Everybody is so relaxed and I think, "God, this could never happen with my family."*

Ken 32   *My father is not accepting. I don't feel my father will really ever change his mind, unless we have a knock down, drag out, fist fight about it. If I want to have a relationship with him, I have to leave out* *certain things and one of them is, I can't ever mention me being gay or my life with Steve. I don't think I could carry on a conversation with someone without mentioning Steve if I'm talking about my daily life. I say "we" went camping or "we" went to the movies. It's not any different than he would do with him and his wife. I cannot compromise in that way. He said basically, "If you continue carrying on with this, I will disown you." and I said "Well then, I'll just end this for you right now," and I hung up. That was three years ago.*

Q   Does that hurt?

Ken   *Yeah, I think it does, but I look at him as another human being that I don't have to like just because he's my father. Maybe that's a rationalization in my brain and that's the only way I can handle it. Maybe on his death bed we will change our ways. I hope that someday he can experience my life now and see how happy I am.*

Q   But doesn't he want to see you happy?

Ken   *I think his desire in life is for him to be happy and everything else is second after that.*

Steve 30   *I was a little more secretive in previous relationships and didn't give my parents the opportunity to be involved. Now that I have, they've really surprised me about how supportive they are. They really like Ken a lot. They want me to be happy. I'm sure, given the choice, if they could choose my life and what I did, they wouldn't choose my life-style now, but since it's made me happy they're very supportive.*

Ken   *Every year his family draws names out of a hat for Christmas gifts and now they've added Steve and Ken, instead of just Steve.*

Steve   *That's such a simple little thing, but it means so much because it validates your relationship. They put our relationship on the same level as my married sister.*

Ken   *It's great to be accepted in a family.*

———————❤———————

Steve 37   *My mother calls up and whines. I ignore her. She's better now.*

Chuck 38   *She's a whining Jewish mother. His mother tries to be accepting of the relationship and she wants to be progressive. She's from an academic background. She's always been around a lot of gay people, but she still can't get over her own cultural stuff. When she visited here and stayed with us, she had little comments like, "There's an awful lot of bars on your street." It was a "can't you be more discreet" attitude. "Why do gay people have to be so overt about their relationships?"*

Steve   *My best friends played right into it. They would go up to her and say, "You know, I don't know why Steven has to live on this street,"* *just to wind her up. She's accepting, because she doesn't want to lose me. It's alright, as long as it's not on your block. When it's your own kid, it's something else. When it comes to progress, as far as gay people go, she's still like a lot of people in that generation, in the dark ages. "Why do you have to yell your sexuality out?" ..."Mom, it's a political issue."*

She would prefer I were with a woman. She wants propriety, someone who she can present, who's a family man with a wife and kids. It's very important to her. I come from a very traditional background. She comes up with cockamamy plans like, "Why don't you marry a lesbian?"

Q Why?

Steve *It would look good and I would be respectable. It will look good to the outside world. What really gets her is when I say, "Look, I came out, you and Dad helped me come out. You're both Holocaust survivors of Hitler and you told me, 'Never let anybody, ever, take away your fundamental right to be who you are!'" For them, that was being Jewish. So I said, "I've taken it a step further."*

Chuck *I communicate with my parents about virtually nothing. We talk on the phone about once every two months. The conversation takes about two to four minutes.*

Sandy 35 *My parents just love Annette. They think she's wonderful. My parents live in the city and we're included all the family functions as a couple. Pops just thinks Annette's the best. They haven't always felt that way about me being a lesbian or about a partner I've had in the past. I think that they can see here that there's something that's really going to last forever.*

Annette 32 *There was never a time that they didn't like me. Her folks were always open to get to know me. They realized, that initially, I was a new girlfriend, but there was a change in that relationship. They realized that it was much more serious.*

Sandy *I came out when I was sixteen and now I'm thirty-five. For the first seven years, it was tough. Mom thought it was a phase. Dad thought, "I don't want to deal with it." As the family gets older, my brothers get older, and I get older, and they go off and get married and divorced, and I still see women, finally my parents say, "Maybe there is something to this, maybe it isn't a phase." It's a joke that my mom and I have that this is the longest phase.*

Q What caused them to be accepting?

Sandy *The reality that I would never change and that I would never do anything to hurt anybody and I would never do anything to hurt myself. Parents always have a dream for you. When I speak of my parents, I speak*

*of my father and my stepmother. I've lived with them since I was seven.
My mom lives down south. She doesn't like the whole idea. She wishes
that I'd get married and have a family. My mom was divorced by the time
she was twenty-two and had three kids, so, why in the hell would she
wish that on me? Annette and I are as happy as can be. What more can
you want for your child than to be happy and not to be wanted in five
states?*

Annette   *My parents are not so accepting. They come around
sometimes. My dad has been most supportive. My mother is not
accepting. It's been two years since they've known, so there's been some
progress. At the core, she feels shame in the family. She's very adamant
that she doesn't want anyone else to know. She thinks that it's a very poor
reflection on her and on my parents as a couple. She has expressed
concern that if people in town knew, or if my aunts and uncles knew, that
they would become ostracized. They would have to endure the ridicule
and the talking behind the backs and all the small town talk that goes with
that in the Mid-West.*

*The other side, the issue for her is a religious one. Her feeling about it
is that it's immoral, and therefore, I have made some very bad choices for
myself. My mother feels very pulled between my father who has been
quite supportive, and my sister who has gone off the other end and said in
so many words, that she would never be in the same room with Sandy and
I, that she finds it so repulsive. My mom feels torn between those two,
wanting to do justice to her own sense of what's right and wrong, as well
as wanting to keep some semblance of family and not wanting to sever the
relationship with me or my sister. I really respect how far she's come in
two years.*

*She took a huge step this past summer and negotiated between my
sister and I for Sandy and I to come to their home for Christmas. My sister
and her family will also be there. Two years in, Mom's beginning to think,
"They're really together, they're really going to stay together, this is really
important and maybe there are issues that are more important to our
family than Annette finding love with another woman."*

Sandy   *When the letter came from Annette's mom inviting both of us
home for Christmas, I just started to cry.*

Annette   *Our parents have met each other. My hope is that my mother,
more so than Dad, will come to learn that she's not the only one who has
a daughter who's a lesbian, not the only one who's ever questioned that or
had to struggle with those issues. Although there are people in my home
town who are in similar situations, because of her fear of telling anyone,
she hasn't been able to find any support.*

---❤---

Otto 60 *To a great extent, my folks never talked about it. They more or less ignored it. They accepted Dick as a son and loved him very much but they didn't discuss our relationship openly. His parents, particularly his dad, is about half and half, half in denial and half accepting. He knows that we are gay and sleep together and have for thirty-three years, but he doesn't acknowledge it to other members of the family. It's a non-sequitur. For our age group, it was really a big thing to come out to parents and friends. As a matter of fact, it was not in good taste to do that when we grew up. With younger gay people today, they want to get it out and get it over with earlier on. We grew up in the 40's and 50's when it was not a good thing to do, so we kept it in the closet.*

Dick 60 *It was dangerous.*

Otto *From the beginning, we had a two bedroom house, but one bedroom was always a den or a computer room. We only had one bed in the house. There was no question but we shared that bed. My parents never commented about that. They just ignored that.*

---❤---

Alice 40 *My mom is great. It took time.*

Christmas 42 *Alice's mother came to our reception and she danced with each of us. She gave us an electric blanket with dual controls. That's pretty accepting. She must know we sleep in the same place.*

Alice *I came out fifteen years ago. My mother was horribly upset when I first told her. There was a distance between us. She was really hurt. I'm an only child and my mother is a very devout Catholic. I think she just saw that I was happy, that I was with people that I loved being around, that I had nice friends. I don't think that she totally accepts it, but in her own way she knows that I'm a daughter that really loves her.*

Christmas *I've adopted Alice's mother because my parents aren't like that. My parents are still pissed off about peace marches I was in, in the 60's. They see everything that I do in my life that they don't approve of, as something that I do at them. My family is very dysfunctional. I have two alcoholic parents. I doubt that they ever will be accepting.*

Q Does that hurt?

Christmas *Mother's Day, Father's Day, none of that bothers me. What hurts every year is at the Gay Parade, when I see parents of lesbians and gays go by. I always, always, every year, go up to at least one or two and I give them a big hug and I tell them that I wish that they were my parents.*

---❤---

John 33   *I don't think my family really knows, even though they know we've been roommates for six years. I come from a big family. My brother and a few sisters are excited about it. They've accepted James as part of the family. My parents don't know that we've actually signed up as Domestic Partners, but they would have to be foolish not to know that we are, because we're on our third apartment in six years.*

James 29   *His mother greeted me like I was her son-in-law. She was so warm and sweet. I don't really have any parents.*

Q   Dead?

James   *No, they're just where they are and I'm where I'm at. They couldn't even accept me being gay. I left home when I was eighteen and came here and that was the last we ever heard from each other.*

Q   Does that hurt you?

James   *From time to time, it does. I wouldn't seriously consider going back or getting in touch with them. They're essentially dead to me. There's no support from them. There really wasn't any love.*

I've had ARC for five years. I haven't had any of the major infections. For a time, I couldn't keep any weight on, a cold will last me a few weeks and I'm tired all the time and achy. I've been on AZT for two years and now it's losing its effectiveness. My T-cells, that had been pretty high up in the normal range, are now starting to go back down. It's pretty sure, I'll progress to full blown AIDS after a certain amount of time.

Q   Wouldn't you like your parents to know? Wouldn't that change their feelings?

James   *I don't think so. They probably think that I already got it and died. John's family really accepted me, so I just borrow a family when I need one. I'm the only one that can pick my relatives. You can't choose your relatives, but you can choose your friends.*

John   *My parents are not aware of James' condition.*

Q   How has that affected your relationship?

James   *I had just come from a relationship that lasted three years and I didn't know anybody with AIDS, so I thought that it passed me by. I didn't realize that I was at ground zero. I guess we weren't smart in the beginning about being safe. It was less than a year after we met that I tested positive. Even after that, we just kind of ignored it for a while, until I got sick. It's too hard, when you're twenty-three and hear that you're going to die right when you feel immortal.*

John   *It has affected us in just about every kind of way, financially, socially, sexually. We've pretty much accepted everything about it.*

James   *It was a battle, heavy denial.*

John   *It's made us closer. With a lot of people, they might not even be* *together any more. I denied it myself. I was afraid to get a test. When I finally did, I was so relieved that I was negative and I looked at it as a sign to do what I can for the ones that need doing for. It's frightening. For the first time in my life, I've seriously thought about death. I've never had anyone really close to me die. It's scary. Lately, we don't plan anything. We just do what we want each day at a time, instead of making long term plans. With the way everything is, we still have it pretty good. We're not nearly as bad off as other people. We're pretty thankful. We just enjoy spending the time with each other.*

James *It's hard for me to leave John or to think about going through that physical decline at the end. I don't want him changing my diapers. Somehow, I want to be able to skip that.*

———————————❤———————————

Darien 47 *My family is supporting. We're what people think of as the traditional close Italian family. Sure, there's been moments of anxiety over my chosen life-style.*

Katherine 40 *It started out very cool. I come from a very conservative traditional Mid-West family. The idea was not well received, but as time has gone on and with the birth of our son, it's warming up. One of the things that my mother had said when David was first born was, "I don't consider him my grandson. I will love him, I will treat him like all the other grandchildren in the family, but I don't think of him that way." But, she's come around. She now does consider him her grandson. She came here, she spent time with him. He melted her.*

———————————❤———————————

Richard 30 *My mother always had this attitude, that it's a passing phase when I do something new. I think she still thinks my relationship with Chris and filing for Domestic Partnership is just that. I really have to prove to her sometimes, that this is permanent. They have a problem with me being gay and they would prefer that I would be straight, but they're not going to shut me out of their life because they love me, that's the bottom line.*

Chris 26 *My parents were very upset when they found out that I was gay. I was seventeen. Over the years, we've become extremely close because they've had a chance to learn and open their minds and find out what my life is all about. I wrote a letter to my mother and I told her. I gave her a pamphlet first that was put out by the Gay Center in Atlanta. It was about myths and misconceptions about gay people. I also told her that she could either accept me for the son that I am or reject me, and it was entirely up to her.*

Over time, I think they realized that I was no different than before they knew. One reason that they were so disapproving at first was because they had all these stereotypes and misconceptions in their heads. I'm sure that they would have preferred that I was straight, only for the reason that life would have been a lot easier for me, as far as not being discriminated against. It's not even approval, because if they don't approve, it's still okay. They said, "It's your life and we love you and we will be there for you thick and thin."

———————————❤———————————

Chris 33   *My parents are sorry that they don't have enough money to pay for the wedding, but then again, I have a very evolved family. My parents have known about my homosexuality since they perceived it when I was twelve years old. They sent me to a therapist at that time, not to cure me, but just to get that therapist to do a reality check for them to make sure I was happy, to make sure that this wasn't a struggle for me, that I wasn't in some personal turmoil that this was a symptom of. I didn't know that was their motivation at that time. I think they embraced my identity because they don't care who I am as long as I am happy.*

Lee 33   *My father is presumed dead. He has been missing for a few decades. I haven't spoken to my mother in a number of years, almost as long as the time that I've been out, so I don't know what she thinks. I don't care what she thinks. My family have been my friends and allies in things that I've worked on in the last few years.*

———————————❤———————————

Jane 49   *My family really loves Coni. My father is 81 and my mother is 79. They were more accepting of me because of the kind of work that I am doing. My family began to feel a sense of pride even though they may not understand it. To have been their daughter, the Presbyterian minister, who had wonderful church jobs and now what was she going to do. Being a lesbian, I lost my job in the church. I never thought I would do ministry again. Then we created the Ministry of Light.*

Coni 39   *I came out to my parents in 1980. I flew back to Illinois, spent a week with them and told them the first night. It was a traumatic experience for me and I know also for them. I thought they had some inclination. Apparently, they had pushed it way back. They really fell back on some Fundamentalist Christian stuff, which we had never been growing up. We grew up in the Methodist Church. They threw biblical stuff at me that week.*

When I got back to San Francisco, my mother continued to write to me. They were really difficult letters to take in. For the first two years, I did everything in my power to try to give them information to better inform them past their myths and stereotypes. They were totally unwilling. They chose not to understand anything. They felt the information was satanic, so they wouldn't touch it or read it. They felt it was totally against God's will.

That's what hurts so much, that I try to live my life with integrity and they know that. They helped teach me that. I come to them and tell them something that I'm really trusting them to be able to tell them, in hopes it would draw us closer. It's taken a long time and a lot of effort. They still feel the same way, but they're tolerant. They don't want their friends to know.

—————————❤—————————

Marty 32 *My family's great, really supportive. They were not always that way. I think my being more comfortable with my sexuality and my preference made them change. When I took Sue home for Christmas, it was a statement for me to say, "This is my life. I'm a lesbian. This is the woman I am going to be with and she is a part of who I am and I want you to meet her." It was like a big risk, but they were very accepting. They saw me for who I am.*

I think we go through life and we have walls and we put up barriers and we don't let people see who we really are. I think I was finally comfortable enough to say, "This is Marty, this is who I am." I have never been more happy in my life.

Susan 33 *I lost my mom when I was a teenager and my dad remarried several times. I never came up to my father and said, "I'm a lesbian, this is my life-style." It was never something that was really talked about, but it was just an understanding. He loves Marty. I never felt like he would not accept who I was with, as long as I was happy and that person was good for me.*

Tell me about your child.

Simone 52   *Anne wanted a child. I was forty-something at the time. I realized that there was something there and that there was going to be a child in my life. We chose artificial insemination with an anonymous donor at the Berkeley Sperm Bank.*

Anne 38   *We felt that we should ask the family's permission, because both of Simone's daughters would be a sibling.*

Two years after having Elizabeth, we applied for Simone to legally adopt her and were denied by the Department of Social Services. We sued the State of California and won. They do not allow same sex adoptions. Now, Elizabeth legally has two mothers.

Simone   *I could have adopted her, but Anne would have had to give up her legal rights.*

Q   What problems will she encounter?

Simone   *Ridicule on the playground with peers. The way you combat that is you provide an environment where she has very good self-esteem. She's going to run across some things, things and words that are going to hurt, and I don't know how to protect her from that. It's going to happen if you're fat, if you're black, if you wear glasses, or whatever. You would do the same thing for any child with any sort of handicap.*

Children of gays and lesbians have enough problems. When you're talking about a child that has been created through artificial insemination and a child that has two legal mothers, we have to be in an environment where she can be accepted. She has enough trouble on the playground, but if we were elsewhere, she'd have a lot more trouble. Here, we can create it so that she has a whole support system and there are other kids that are like her.

❦

Rachel 30   *I've always wanted to have a child. I bore the child by artificial insemination with an anonymous donor. We're in this together.*

Joan 45   *As far as my rights with the baby, I don't have any that any court would recognize. In the future, I will adopt the baby, and in the law we will be equal parents of the baby. Domestic Partnership is a little step towards saying that we're in this relationship and I have been with the baby all along.*

Rachel   *There are a number of couples in the Bay Area that have done co-parent adoptions. At this point, she is named in my will as the one I would like to see have the child, but the court can overrule wills on that sort of thing. San Francisco is a more comfortable place, certainly, to raise a child in a non-traditional relationship.*

Joan   *We have a baby who's sick with a lot of ear infections and that's meant a lot of times he couldn't go to day care and one of us had to stay home with him. We take turns, take partial days, trying to work around our jobs to take care of him and lose as little time from work as possible.*

Rachel   *I expect it's really the unusual man who takes on 50% of the child care responsibilities. I have a lot more respect for women that are single parents or women that are doing it with less support from their husbands.*

Kevin 37   *Sarah's three and she's been with us since we were present at her birth. It was a private adoption by both of us.*

Dan 37   *We are one of the few couples that have successfully done that.*

Kevin   *I love children and so does Dan. I really wanted to be a parent. It's wonderful, just another dimension of life.*

Q   Are you going to have more children?

Dan   *Our daughter needs a sibling. It would deflate her little sense of omnipotence and being the center of the universe.*

Katherine 40   *David is the apple of my eye. My whole life long I was destined to be a mother. It was the most enduring wish of my life. I considered the idea for years, even before Darien and I were together. We went to a private physician who does anonymous donor inseminations.*

He's in pre-school here. He's in his second year.

Q   How is it for David to have two moms?

Katherine   *They're wonderful at his school. We were up front from the very beginning that we are a two-mother family. Every time it's Mother's Day or Christmas, there are two mother gifts that he has made.*

Darien 47   *There are other gay parents there.*

Katherine   *Because of our Domestic Partnership, David will take comfort and umbrage that this is an officially sanctioned family.*

Darien   *And that others whom he respects and loves treat it that way. People know that we're two mommies raising David. Some of our best friends are some of our neighbors.*

What about the opposition?

John 35   *They're looking to discredit that we exist.*
Richard 37   *I think it's mostly homophobia. It's unsaid but there seems to be this threat. This concept of traditional values; there isn't really much more of a traditional value than people wanting to start a family and a home together whether the family is two people with no children or people with children. It's still family and making a home and caring for each other. It's really a very private thing.*

David 45   *We see Domestic Partnership as a step in the right direction and they see it as a step in the wrong direction. I think in ten years there will be marriages like there is in Sweden and Denmark. The right wing sees it as the first step and if you don't fight that first step, it's hard to fight the next step.*
David 40   *They have never recognized that gay people exist or should have the right. With AIDS, gay people are sticking out in the crowd and they're finding out that we're all over the place. I feel the stereotypical traditionalists say that we don't have permanent relationships, we don't bond for longer than a night or a week or a month.*

Lori 28   *People are afraid. There are so many people that think we're sick and weirdos. I look at my family and some of the things they've said. We were great friends up until the moment I told them about Anita. There are people out there like that, that forget that you're a human being and just think you're a sick freak, a pervert that should have no rights whatsoever, that you shouldn't even exist.*
Anita 35   *Or we can exist, but behind closed doors. "Don't flaunt it in front of us."*
Lori   *They think that if they let their kids talk to us or watch us that all of a sudden they're going to be gay.*

Harry 63   *It's a toe hold.*
Jack 60   *It's a threat. These preachers that are preaching against us don't give a damn what we do as long as we don't broadcast it and as long as it is not accepted. They're unsure of themselves. It's frightening to them and their scale of values. They don't understand homosexuality and gayness. If it were limited to men and women, they wouldn't be fighting it. You can't be blind to the fact that this is an anti-gay movement. No one's ever yelled about common law marriage. If it were completely a*

straight issue, there would be no groups of religious fanatics against it.
They are frightened of homosexuality.

———————————❤———————————

Gwynn 28   *Homophobia. People are afraid of anybody who is outside*
their realm of experience, and that doesn't matter whether they're gay or
Jewish or black or Asian.

Bert 45   *If this is religion and this is the church and it's love thy*
neighbor and do unto others, what is the big objection? We're all human
beings. We have a lot of things in common. The only thing that seems to
be different would be sexual preference. When you stop and think about
what the true teachings of the bible are, they're about brotherly love,
they're about taking care of one another, about unconditional love, and
forgiving everybody. That's the basic teaching. Men got in the way and
fucked it up, then they started doing all of their different interpretations.
We have our Fundamentalist interpretation and we have our Jewish
interpretations and we have our Muslim and all the others. Then, they
started adding all the man stuff, stuff that came out of their own head.

The thing with Gwynn's family is no matter how much they love him,
and they genuinely do, in their Bible, in their church that they participate
in, homosexuality is a sin...period...the end. So, they're really wrestling
with this whole issue of, "How do we love our son and stay true to the
church." As hard as it has been for Gwynn and me on this end, I honestly
have to believe in my heart that it's been harder for them on their end,
because they're trying to resolve these two very conflicting things. How
do they stay true to the God that they believe in? Somebody just wrote
that in a book and they bought it.

Gwynn   *One reason we're not out trying to pass laws to end whatever*
they're doing is because you know where that has come from, because
you were raised by heterosexual people. I don't agree with it, but they
have the right to their opinion.

———————————❤———————————

William 62   *Ignorance.*

Roderick 57   *It's the religious right. I think that they're frustrated gays*
themselves. They just hate to see anybody live their lives and be happy
because they can't. I'm sure they're not all gay, the religious
fundamentalists, but I think there are a lot among them that are just
frustrated gays.

William   *We saw Cardinal O'Connor telling his parish "Don't you*
accept them because they are hateful." These people are not hateful. The
religious groups twist this around that they hate us, so we've got to hate

them, or we should hate them.

Roderick   *It is the religious faction that's doing it, which is creating a hate factor with the gay community. Gays don't trust churches anymore.*

Roderick   *When I was a teenager, if you were gay, you kept your mouth shut. If you wanted to make contact, you had to have a certain movement, a certain flair that told other gays that you were a gay person. That's where the limp wrist comes from. If you're in San Francisco, you don't see that much of that. The further east you go in the small towns where young gays come up, they are doing exactly the same thing that I was doing when I was a youth in this city before the freedoms came in. You had to express yourself, so you became feminine as a male and a woman, a lesbian, had to be very butch... take butch jobs, whereas the new lesbians that are coming in today are much more feminine. What do they call them, lipstick dykes or something?*

Q   What do you think will change the stereotypical view of gays?

William   *The one-on-one, like your personal friend that you've known for years and respect and you find out he's gay. I think that's the best way for the public to become educated.*

—————————❤—————————

Anonymous 46   *They're on to us. They know that what we'd like to do is give it teeth.*

Q   What about the objection to Domestic Partners being on City Health Insurance?

Anonymous 46   *People have no objection at all to married couples being in on their partners' health benefits...none. When it gets down to gay couples...it's absurd...it's just another human being.*

Anonymous 37   *One of the things that moves the American population on a large scale is financial worries. If you start telling people, in the middle of a recession, people who are at risk of losing their jobs, that something is going to cost them a large amount of money, it's a very effective tool...whether it's true or it's not true.*

Anonymous 46   *People want to feel better than other people. People want to feel that they are superior to some one. There are certain groups that have been labeled as inferior, certain races and definitely queers are not as good as you and I or whoever. It is very deeply disturbing to people to be told that my relationship is just as good as theirs and I'm going to have the same rights. It is just more than they can stand.*

Most people are not clear about who they are sexually. Most people are heterosexual and they're okay. "I'm okay, I'm a real man or a real woman, I have this other person in my life that validates that I have a husband or a wife and that validates me. I'm okay." If you go around and start telling them that you're queer it brings up in them "Oh my God, what if I'm like that. I can't deal with that, so I don't want to deal with you."

Anonymous 37   *I think that they think it's bad to be sexual, period. It's not necessarily that homosexuality in itself is so bad, it's that sexuality in itself is bad.*

Anonymous 46   *We come from a puritanical, Judeo-Christian, bureau-centric system of morality. We hate our bodies; we hate our sexuality. We pent that up. It's still there.*

Anonymous 37   *People tend to live their lives with not really being honest with who they are and what they're about. People like to think that they are generous and fair and have principles that they live their life by and if you really dissect anybody, the bottom line is that there's a little bit of evil and badness in everybody. People lie; people don't stand up for the principles that they think they believe in.*

People pass homeless people on the street and look the other way and then go to church and talk about loving thy brother. It runs through human psychology and sexuality. They're not in touch with it. They don't acknowledge it. They're scared to hell of it. Part of the big threat of gay people is that when a person is labeled as a homosexual, the whole term talks about their sexuality.

They're not looking at who we are. They don't want to know what our relationship is. They only thing that they're interested in is that we're both women and we sleep with each other and we make love with each other. That's what the fear is based on. If they get to know us individually or together, we're not threatening, we're just people like everybody else. You see two women walking together with their arms around each other and it suddenly brings up images of sex.

Anonymous 46   *People used to be in couples all the time. You read about it historically. There were loving friends of both sexes that would live together for 40 or 50 years and no problem. The second you call attention to the fact that there is a sexual aspect to this relationship, people go nuts.*

Anonymous 37   *The reason people oppose anything having to do with Domestic Partnership is because of financial issues, but I think it goes a lot deeper than that. It has to do with people's fundamental terror of recognizing alternative relationships and recognizing the fact that the nuclear family, that some people feel is the ideal norm of the American population, has never really existed as a norm or an average.*

The same people that are fighting against Domestic Partnership refuse to believe that the divorce rate is as high as it is and that people commit infidelity within a traditional heterosexual marriage as often as they do. There are a hell of a lot of other people in this world that live in family structures, grandparents raising children, unmarried couples living together, old people that have no legal bonds that are in joint living situations. There are a lot of non-traditional couples and this terrifies people.

❤

Gwen 26 *It scares them. They think that it does ape marriage. They don't think that there should be homosexuals at all, let alone recognized homosexual relationships.*

❤

Joel 47 *It's because of the religious right wing who feel they need a cause, and certainly sinning is a cause. Homosexuality is a sin and even the straight Domestic Partners who registered are just as sinful because they are not married in the eyes of God.*

Tony 39 *There is some opposition to costs or alleged costs. It's unequal right now. It's unfair for a co-worker to sign a paper and get health insurance for their spouse at less than a Domestic Partner is able to get health insurance.*

Q Religion teaches us to love thy neighbor, to forgive...

Joel *Only if you cure yourself, cure your homosexuality, then you may be forgiven. It's the stereotypical way of looking at life and that's probably what the religious right wing does. All they see are the flaming queens and the bull dykes. Those are the only people that are visible. One thing Domestic Partnership may help to change is that maybe in some way, people will see that we're just ordinary people.*

❤

Eric 29 *The main argument was that it goes against everything the family is about. Most of the people opposing it have a very narrow view of family. Families are definitely evolving and changing constantly. Within that last twenty years there's been a definite trend toward unrelated people living together in families.*

❤

Hugh 46 *People fail to realize that Domestic Partnership is not just for gays and lesbians, that it is for any couple living together.*

David 40 *Homophobia, ignorance, fear, feeling threatened by the unknown.*

❤

Wade 34 *People want to think about gay relationships in terms of sex and not in terms of love. Most of the focus is on the gay couples, not the straight couples. I think it's particularly threatening, in the sense that, what it's talking about is caring. I think that they're opposed to the thought that gay people have caring relationships. Society wants to say that they have perverse sexual relationships, not loving relationships.*

Brent 38 *It is from the Judeo-Christian tradition. It says it right in the Bible. Even people who are not religious are brought up in that tradition. You can't escape the fact that this society is based on some kind of Christian religion.*

I think a lot of people see Domestic Partnership as a first step of validating homosexual behavior. A lot of people object to that. This is the tip of the iceberg and people will be asking for more and more rights, and they see that as a threat. Prejudice is based on the fear of the unknown.

Steve 49 *They're so bent out of shape about anybody loving in a way different from the way they love. They're taught in their churches that there is only one way to live your life and they can't accept anyone living differently.*

Dan 40 *Homophobia. One misconception, that a lot of the homophobic population has, is that they think we lead these really bizarre, weird life-styles, when in reality most gays just lead a normal everyday life-style like everyone else. Their relationships are pretty much just like other relationships in many ways. There are wild and crazy and extreme gays and there are wild and crazy and extreme heterosexuals with all sorts of defined or loosely defined relationships.*

Helene 39 *It is somehow giving societal sanction to homosexual couples. The vast majority of people that file for Domestic Partnership are gay and lesbian couples because we ain't got no other option. We can't say, "Well, we could be Domestic Partners or we could get married or we could not be anything." The only option we have is to legally not be anything or to have this little bit of symbolic thing called registering as Domestic Partners. Some straight people are doing that and that should be an option for them.*

Kit 39 *It boils down to homophobia.*

Q What would change their minds?

Helene *Nothing.*

Kit *Sometimes I think it's out of ignorance, out of believing a lot of myths that aren't reality for most gays and lesbians in this country. In* *some cases it could be education, but in some cases people base it on religious convictions or very deeply held beliefs that education isn't going to change. If somebody quotes the Bible at you and it says that it's a sin in the sight of God, you can educate them until you are blue in the face and it's not going to make any difference.*

Q   Why do you think the opposition holds such a stereotypical view of the gay and lesbian community and homophobia?

Helene   *In a lot of places, they get that from the media. It prints things that are news and that get people's attention. Kit and I getting up in the morning and going to work, me in a law office and her doing computer stuff, that's not news. But some outrageous drag queen is news because there's the shock value for the average American in Iowa.*

It has made a difference in the way Kit's parents view us as a couple to have them spend several days here and get to see that what they thought of as stereotypes. A lot of their fears about their daughter being a lesbian were not a reality. We weren't alone and isolated, we had gay and lesbian friends, straight friends, co-workers, etc. Basically, our lives were a lot healthier and a lot richer than their fears were. It made a lot of difference.

---❤---

Lauren 29   *People are afraid of legitimizing gay relationships.*

Jane 29   *If the ordinance gave us the right of insurance or gave us a lot of financial protection, the thing that people would still be most afraid of is that it legitimizes this relationship as a family.*

Lauren   *It's having society say that our relationship is okay and I don't think society is ready to say that.*

Jane   *Not even San Francisco society, apparently. They believe that it threatens the existence of the American family. I guess I've been in this life-style so long that I can't even empathize with their opinions any more.*

Q   How can you change the opposition?

Jane   *You change it by coming out. You put your name on the dotted line at City Hall and not be afraid of the repercussions by being out in the workplace. We've accomplished as much being out in our workplaces as ACT UP does in any demonstration on the TV. People ask me questions and they see how normal I am and they're not threatened by my life-style. Just hang out and be as normal as possible.*

Lauren   *Homosexuals are faceless. They don't know the lesbians and gays. I tell them at work that I'm gay and they die. But then after that they come back and ask stupid questions like, "What do you do in bed?" or "Who's the man?" or "Who plays what role?" I don't leave it open so that they will ask those questions anymore. Maybe it's my maturity.*

─────────────────❤─────────────────

Brad 30   *Fear, fear of change.*

Carl 46   *It tends to give credence to non-traditional marriages which the vast majority of the population is against.*

Q   What do you think will cause the opposition to change?

Brad   *Familiarization. If their son or daughter or brother or sister were to be gay and still be their brother or sister and they could have a pleasant dinner with them or a nice conversation.*

Carl   *Things will change when we stop riding in the back of the bus and we let people see who we are, how we are and what we are and how we live and not just the bits and pieces that they see in news magazines or on television about ACT UP or Queer Nation or the more extreme Left. Most of us are pretty okay people like everybody else. We have middle income salaries and we eat the same foods and we like fresh salmon when you can get it at under $10 per pound. We go out to movies and we exercise.*

Brad   *AIDS scares the heterosexual population. They figure by saying no to Domestic Partnership it will go away. Domestic Partnership ought to help that since it's sex with a single partner.*

Carl   *I don't know what relationship AIDS would have with Domestic Partnership.*

─────────────────❤─────────────────

Richard 28   *The church and religion have a lot to do with it. They're afraid of it breaking down the traditional family values, their traditional man/woman/children thing.*

Wally 37   *There's nothing non-traditional about our commitment. What's so difficult is that people still do not know and understand homosexuality because they're being continuously fed by some very old and ancient dogma.*

Richard   *Religion, a lack of knowledge and some people are just scared by it. People are also scared when they see things that they don't like in themselves.*

Wally   *People are generally scared by what they don't know. Fear gets the best of people. Fear is generated by ignorance. Every gay person has been a victim of some sort of discrimination, whether it's been a beer bottle being thrown at them when they're walking down the street or a snippy remark from some secretary.*

How come so many straight people that I know who live in San Francisco and have been around lots of gay men and gay women seem to have no problem with it? The reason is that they have been around gay people. They know that they're not a threat to them. They're comfortable with their own sexuality.

Richard *They know that we're not out to steal their husbands and rape their children.*

Wally *I think it happens only in major metropolitan areas, like New York, Chicago, Los Angeles, and San Francisco. As soon as you move in to the Bible belt with preachers, people tend to be of lower incomes and think that they have to turn to their church for their social events, security, and support in their lives. Nothing exists except their little town in Iowa.*

❤

Jay 41 *It just doesn't sit right with them.*

Lotus just gave all the partners health benefits, unmarried and same sex, because they said straight people have the option to get married and get the benefits. That is a big deal. Lotus did it first. Nobody wanted to be first. They're a big company and boy are they getting good PR over that. When people "back in America" read it they think, "Yeah, why not?"

Q   What do you mean people "back in America?"

Jay *Any place outside of here, we call " back in America."*

Ken 45 *The ordinance, as it stands now, is pretty bland. It has no financial burden on the taxpayers at all, so what's the problem, what are they afraid of, other than that which dare not speak its name.*

Jay *If it were just for unmarried heterosexuals, they probably wouldn't be doing what they're doing now. It wouldn't be on the ballot again, not at all. I don't think it's against the Domestic Partners Ordinance, I think it's just against gay people.*

❤

Anne 38 *There's radical homophobia. There are people who believe that we do not have a right to exist.*

Simone 52 *I have come to the point to believe that they are just very evil. They know better, but they just won't let go of the hatred. I'm not talking about the little lady in Kansas who doesn't know anything, that's never been exposed, but the people who should know better.*

Anne *We're talking about religious, not spiritual groups and certainly not Christian groups, not what I define as Christian. Good Christian people certainly don't use hateful and deceitful practices. They got the message out through the pulpit, through flyers placed on telephone poles. It's American society's aversion to sexuality in general...gay sex , straight sex, kid sex.*

Simone *The gay and lesbian life-style is not about sex. It's a whole way of thinking and feeling. When the opposition was age two, they got* *the same impressions as we got. The message is very subtle. Somehow through the power of advertising...you don't see men and men in a Vodka ad, you wouldn't see two lesbians sitting down in an ad for Nescafé. These messages are given to you that everything is heterosexual sex.*

❤

Steve 35   *There's just as much opposition to it as we are excited about it. It's a very small thing, but it's the symbolism of it. It opens the door that much and it might make it a little bit easier the next time to pass something like bereavement leave or medical coverage to a significant other.*

Phillip 27   *They realize that a domino has fallen..."God help us all, gay marriage is around the corner and before you know it, they'll have the same rights as everybody and God forbid that."*

❤

Rachel 30   *Socially and religiously conservative people are threatened by giving any kind of legitimacy to our relationships. They're probably threatened by heterosexual couples as well.*

❤

Lynn 38   *Bottom line, the opposition stems from homophobia, especially as it's found in the more fundamentalist religious community. Certainly those folks object to unmarried heterosexual couples but there's a quantum leap between their level of objection to gay relationships.*

Jackie 40   *Discrimination against people or behaviors that are not understood. They're perceived as different and bad.*

❤

Adria-Ann 43   *The basic issue is really a moral issue. I certainly don't see myself as a threat. I'm a productive lady and I feel good about myself and about Kris. I feel certain that if any of those people met me personally and talked to me that they wouldn't find me personally objectionable.*

Kris 26   *Any kind of equal status is just too threatening. In a lot of cases, people are reacting against their own insecurities and fears.*

❤

Larry 45   *It comes from right wing, Fundamentalist type people who are deeply anti-gay, among many other things. They don't want us to have any rights; they don't like our relationships; they don't like our sexuality; they don't want us to exist; they would rather we be dead or off the face of the earth. For us to affirm our love for each other and say that it's good in City Hall, the seat of government, is obnoxious to them. They don't like homosexual people because we don't fit into their narrow little idea of how people should live. They want the nuclear family to be the center of* *everything and male dominated. They get a lot of it from the Bible and from centuries of patriarchy.*

Wood 45 *They fear us, that's why they call it homophobia. They fear that they may lose status if they're associated with us and they also gain status by putting us down. In our society there are few things worse than being a homosexual. If you're straight, you can always say, "Well, at least I'm not a queer." They can always say that no matter how rotten their marriage is, if they beat their wives, if they hate each other, they can always say, "I'm not a queer." When we come out and we show that we have love, that negates that part. They can't logically say any more, "I'm better than a queer."*

———————❤———————

Steve 30 *Ignorance breeds fear. Most of them didn't take the time to read the ordinance, they just hopped on a band wagon. It would validate a homosexual relationship.*

Ken 32 *To the religious Fundamentalists homosexuality is a sin, so, do not support anything that furthers the cause of homosexuality.*

Steve *Unmarried, opposite sex partners are also a sin to them. They're afraid. One of the names of these groups is the Traditional Values Coalition. If they had their way, we'd be back to June and Ward Cleaver.*

———————❤———————

Richard 34 *It still offends so many people that two same sex people can love each other. They hate the thought of two people of the same sex having sex together, but when the question of love comes in, it challenges them. They think, "Oh my God, these aren't the horrible things we thought they were, and they're just like us."*

Hugh 51 *Most of the opposition has come from the right wing Christian block. I am a Christian. I do not impose my beliefs on anybody. I don't wear them on my sleeve. They are very important to me. My God is one of love not of hate. Their reaction is a hateful one in the name of God. The Bible says that homosexuality is an abomination. It also says that the Lord reigns on the just and the unjust.*

I operate on a principle of loving people, not hating them. It is disturbing to me when I hear this outpouring of hate from the so-called Christians. I don't know what will convince them that our relationship is as valid as theirs might be with their mates. The thing that's really bothered me about the criticism of the gay community is that they seem to focus on what gay people do in the bedroom. I have absolutely no business asking anyone what they do in the bedroom. Sex seems to be the focus. That is not what gay relationships or heterosexual relationships or non-married relationships are all about.   It is not a sex question to us.   We love each other.

———————————❤———————————

Jeanette 37   *Clearly, homophobia.*

Stephanie 48   *It's threatening the traditional values.   That's threatening the tenets of the church.   Not only is it promiscuity, but same-sex sex. Marriage is becoming obsolete and there's all kinds of taboos being broken.*

Stephanie   *Because there has to be a specific law around gays and lesbians, it shows how much discrimination exists.   The most poignant tales are around gay men who are not allowed in the hospitals of their lovers who are dying or who can't take a day off work for a funeral because it's not considered a relative.   Those are the issues that brought this to the floor.   They're not written into the bill, but it feels like the first step.*

———————————❤———————————

Jeff 38   *Right wing fanatic religious groups that see unwed couples of any kind living together as being blasphemous.*

———————————❤———————————

Kevin 37   *Fear and the constant misunderstanding of who we are as gay and lesbian people.   It's primarily seen as an attack against the family structure.   It has nothing to do with all those nice heterosexual people who just haven't made the big step to get married yet.*

———————————❤———————————

Steve 37   *Any kind of inroad that makes gay relationships even remotely resemble a social contract like heterosexual relationships that can be validated through marriage is extremely threatening to traditional forces in society.   Anything that has any glimmer of that would raise quite an uproar.*

Chuck 38   *The power of the legislation is really in its symbolism, just as the power in marriage is mostly in its symbolism.   That power is exactly what the opposition was opposed to.*

Steve   *It's the typical Catch 22 that happens with trying to legalize gay relationships.   The homophobes say that we're incapable of stable relationships, but of course, we are.   When gay people want those validated through marriage, they say, "Sorry, you can't get married."   So, we're in a double bind.   We want to sanctify and legitimize our relationships legally and we're told we can't do that.   We're being damned if we do and damned if we don't.*

———————————❤———————————

Annette 32 *I don't understand what the fear is about. In my mind, having met Sandy and fallen in love with her is what I'm about in this world. It was what was supposed to happen. Growing up I always heard, although the stereotype was that I was supposed to do this with a man, that I was supposed to find that special someone and that I was supposed to settle down with them and we were supposed to build a life together and have a family together and that society would approve of that and sanction that.*

There are stories of acceptance of the two older women who lived down the road in their own house. You think of them as sisters or best friends. But two men living together all of a sudden raises all these suspicions. They think they're out to proselytize everybody in town or that they're molesters or criminals. They perceive homosexuality as being a male thing.

There's a component that says that homosexuality is an illness, that it's either a mental disorder or a biological, genetic disorder of sorts that needs to be cured, that needs treatment; or given some interpretations of the Judeo-Christian tradition, that it would be perceived as being immoral.

❤

Dick 60 *Fear. People who are homophobic are fundamentally afraid of their own selves. They're trying to control others because they're afraid if there are no controls that they themselves will go wild.*

Otto 60 *They're afraid of losing the nuclear family cohesiveness that has been around for years and years. It's not a valid fear as far as gay persons are concerned. We didn't choose to be gay, we happen to be gay. We have to make our families understand that we need relationships and we can build our own families very often by choosing those people that we want to be associated with in our own little extended family group. It's important for all people to be part of a family, whether or not it's the traditionally nuclear family.*

Dick *It's almost religious. Why, for centuries, did the church fight any changes whatsoever in anything? That's something that puzzles scholars today. The sociological interpretation is that there's a fear of the loss of traditional values. The psychological interpretation is that there's a fear of the loss of control.*

Surely you've heard someone say, "If we legitimize gay relationships there won't be any children, that if homosexuality is legitimized everyone will be homosexual." This is the external fear they express. It's not a rational fear, but it's a real fear. Where can they possibly get such a fear but from themselves?

They must internally be afraid that if homosexuality is legitimized that

*they will become homosexuals. That has to be what their fear is. They're
externalizing that by saying that's what's going to happen to everyone
else.*

❤

Christmas 42   *It challenges the status quo of people who have always
been the role models for the universe. If you present an alternative, it gets
people thinking that you don't have to do it the same way. Love comes in
a lot of different shapes and shades. Nobody has a trademark on family.
There are so many types of family that are not represented by what
actually doesn't exist as a majority any more. There are many more single
parent families.*

*They don't want to see us as having stable relationships. They prefer
the image of people who are running around fucking like bunnies. They
can look at that and say, "See, they're immoral, they aren't families, they
don't have a right to be recognized as a legitimate stable family unit."
Those are the same people who don't want choice for women. It doesn't
surprise me that they don't want choice for anybody else in a lot of other
areas.*

Alice 40   *I think they need to open up their minds and their hearts and
see beyond themselves to see that there's other ways of doing things.*

❤

James 29   *People were worried about their taxes going up, with sharing
insurance, especially when it comes to gay men, a lot of whom are sick.
They thought it would be a big drain. It's going to be a big drain on them
anyway, no matter what. Domestic Partnership turned out to be just like
common law marriage that straight people have had since the beginning.
Different factions don't want to be anything like the straight community
with anything like marriage.*

❤

Darien 47   *There are people that have this fear that these kinds of
relationships are destroying the family environment. Families in America
are falling apart for a lot of reasons. That Katherine and I choose to live
together with our son David as family, is not the reason why families are
falling apart out there.*

❤

Todd 27   *The far right doesn't want to believe that gays and lesbians are
capable of sustaining long term relationships. First of all, they believe that
it's sinful or maybe immoral.*

Ben 32   *In this age, you would think that the State would want to
promote stable relationships because of AIDS. You would want to*

*promote monogamy. Why is racism such a great part of our society even
today? Some people hate and have a great deal of hate in their blood.
They can't purge themselves of it, so they find outlets like beating up gays
or being racists. It's a real sad commentary on our society.*

---❤---

Chris 26   *It is so very little, but it is one step in the process. A lot of the
opposition is the religious Fundamentalists, the ultra-conservatives. A lot
of them are misled.*

Richard 30   *Because they think that it is saying publicly that it is okay
to endorse non-marriage relationships. But, for most Fundamentalists who
read the Bible, it is not okay. Not just Christians, but Jews and Buddhists.
It's very threatening for us to be granted rights and freedoms. They don't
like us and they don't approve of how we live.*

Chris   *The Bible has been used throughout history to condemn blacks
and women and even in the 40s it was used to justify the persecution of
Jews. Now it's being used against the gay community. It's part of human
nature to be afraid of what is different than what you grew up with and
have been taught all of your life. A lot of people are in this safe shell and
this little mold and it scares them to see something different. It makes
them look at themselves as well.*

---❤---

Chris 33   *Because we're not heterosexual and only having sex that the
woman doesn't care about in the missionary position to produce children.
Any affirmation at any level of any relationship other than the one that fits
that mold is absolutely abhorrent to those people. Heterosexual couples
are still outside of the covenant of marriage.*

*There are churches in the world that do not sanction any of the people
that went down there to file an alternative relationship. I don't think any
of the opposition leaders belong to any churches that sanction alternative
relationships other than those that have been blessed by the god of their
choosing. I really think this is about religion.*

Lee 33   *I think there is a very narrow window of what is okay. They
want to believe that the world should exist that way and that homosexuals
are sick and should not exist.*

---❤---

Coni 39   *The opposition states that lesbian and gay people are not to
be classified as a minority group because we don't deserve to have a
minority status. We are classified as sinful. I'm talking about the people
who probably object most. It comes from Christianity. They take certain
biblical passages that appear in the Bible. They don't apply to us in the*

way they are taking them and the way that they have been taken for centuries now. There are seven passages that we refer to as "clobber passages" that have been used to hit us over the head with, repeatedly, to tell us that we are inherently evil. These passages have been translated into English saying things like, "You shall not lie with a woman as you do with a man, if you're a woman." The Sodom and Gomorrah story is usually cited as one of the instances. They cite the biblical text in Genesis that woman was made to be with man as man's helpmate. That is the only possible romantic relationship that is to be sanctioned ever.

They say that you should only have sex after marriage. That's not in the Bible. It goes back to the roots of patriarchy where there's an imbalance of power between men and women. It's an attempt to keep the status quo and men in the power place. It's very much related to sexism. Sexism, heterosexism, and racism are very entwined together.

Jane 49   It's based on dualism where the body is bad and the spirit is good.

Coni   Men are better than women; white people are better than people of color; straight people are better than lesbian and gay people. This is seen to so jeopardize the family, that if we were to be given equal rights or sanction, it would destroy the family.

They don't see Domestic Partnership as stabilizing us. What is acceptable is to change us. If they can put their energies into changing us from being lesbian or gay to being straight, then that's a victory. They think we choose this behavior, so all we have to do is un-choose it. They think the only way to be a positive member of society is to be heterosexual.

❤

Marty 32   I think the people most opposed to it are afraid that this is a first step toward real legalization of lesbian and gay marriages and other types of non-traditional families. I think people are frightened of that.

Susan 33   It's not the norm that the society has grown up with. You have to have the man, a woman and children and your job and your house and the white picket fence. This is not the norm and people are afraid to say, "Maybe it's okay." They're very judgemental. I think a lot of people just see the bad side of the spectrum, what the media shows when they show a gay or lesbian event.

Marty   There are numerous gay and lesbian couples that are very professional, that work as lawyers, doctors, paramedics, and nurses, and have families. Those people are boring...not the ones that make the news.

What about the future?

Anita 35   *I think it will still be the same.*

Lori 28   *I don't. I really don't. There's so many issues going on, the big military stuff, the outing thing.*

Anita   *I think the Fundamentalists are coming on strong and they really want to tell us what we can and can't do. I think they're going to get more and more powerful with abortion, with gay rights. I don't think we'll ever be accepted. I will be pleasantly surprised if we are.*

All we can do is do our little part to show that gay couples can live normal, healthy lives just like everybody else. We can represent this for ourselves and our community and the small segment of people we encounter. As a whole, I think there's still that big part of middle America that wants to tell us what to do.

William 62   *I don't think the Federal Government's going to have anything to do with it. It's going to be a state-by-state thing and it's going to be modeled after Denmark.*

Roderick 57   *Within our lifetime, we're going to see the military accepting gays as gays. As far as recognizing gay marriage, that won't come in our lifetime.*

William   *There are too many opposing people that are ignorant. It will take an education.*

Roderick   *The extreme religious Fundamentalists have too much influence. We need to start getting our act together in this country. We back others individual rights, but we don't have rights of our own. Changes are coming, like airlines, a spouse gets to go half fare and now a partner can go, or a friend.*

Steve 45   *Marriage laws are a matter for each individual state and not the Federal Government. It's conceivable that there would be changes in regard to the tax laws.*

Helene 39   *In the last few years, more places have passed Domestic Partnership. The trend has been more toward acceptance, or tolerance at least. The bad state of the economy usually causes a more conservative trend. There's fewer jobs and you're less likely to be as accepting of women and racial minorities and whatever. My fear is that there may be a type of a backlash to some of the good stuff that has already happened. It will take a long time before the Federal Government does anything. It will* *be way beyond the year 2000.*

What has happened lately has partly been because more gay and lesbian people have been willing to take the risk of being out publicly in their own neighborhoods and work situations. There have been such events as the 1987 March on Washington which have been extremely empowering for people that went to that and then came home to work more in their local areas and make some of that become a reality.

More of us need to be out in more places, then it will be harder for people to stereotype. If you know somebody who is gay or lesbian, and they happen to be somebody that you work with or somebody that lives in your neighborhood and you can see that they mow their lawn, that they do a good job at work, then I think that breaks down a lot of the stereotype. That's the kind of stuff that's going to help. That's going to have to come before the legal stuff.

---❤---

Carl 36   *I don't know. I would hope that we could continue to demonstrate and make inroads step-by-step to ultimately be as fully recognized as any other couple.*

Brad 30   *I'd like to go to the ballet or the opera and not really be noticed or eyebrowed.*

Carl   *Discrimination by any name is still hate. I think we have enough years of that in our human history that we can look at it and not want to participate in it any more.*

---❤---

Lauren 29   *I see a lot of same-sex parents. I'm seeing children's books come out with two fathers, two moms and I'm loving it. Jane and I want to have a child and by that time I want to make sure the environment is somewhat safe. I don't want my child to be ostracized.*

Jane 29   *You're going to see a lot more gays and lesbians in traditional, straight institutions. There will be a lot of dykes in the PTA and a lot of top notch gay politicians.*

---❤---

Richard 28   *It will take getting the old out and bringing in some new blood, plus education.*

Wally 37   *Getting the media to show something other than drag queens as a representation of what gay people are.*

Richard   *Anytime you turn on a TV program about gay people, they have a drag queen representing the man and to represent the women, they have something that weighs about 400 lbs., has a crew cut, and wears a motorcycle jacket.*

Wally   *Those are extremes in our community. I don't think it's an accurate representation. I put on a suit and tie and go to work everyday, come home, and I go to the gym. I lead a very regular life-style.*

Richard   *I put on a uniform and steel toed shoes and go in and throw around 150 lb. packages.*

❤

Ken 45   *I want to say that it will be better and that the Lotus example will be followed by quite a few more companies. Business will probably be ahead of Government in terms of recognizing non-traditional families.*

Jay 41   *Here's this huge company Lotus giving health benefits to same sex couples that work for their company and it's on the Governor's desk to sign the anti-discrimination bill. Look how far we've come.*

I remember going out as a gay kid, almost thirty years ago. We had to knock three times on the door to the bars to get in the back door and here we're walking down City Hall stairs as Domestic Partners in a major city in the United States.

❤

Simone 52   *We have to come out. I was a lesbian in 1976, in a relationship with another woman. I was in Paris and it was the first time I saw other women touching and kissing and I couldn't believe my eyes. I had never seen anything like that. I was shocked. It was like, "Oh my God, they're kissing in public." There was a part of me that was embarrassed, I felt awkward, I wanted them to stop. We have our own homophobia. We're taught that you're not supposed to do that. Now, of course, I've been exposed to it. They can be kissing right here outside my door and it doesn't mean anything.*

Anne 38   *We have to come out. If everybody in Kansas or Michigan or wherever, sees that in addition to their hair dresser and maybe their lady plumber being gay or lesbian, that also their teacher, their C.P.A., their floor waxer, and their bank president is gay. If all of us who are gay and lesbian woke one morning and had green hair and went out into the street and everybody said, "Oh gosh, they have green hair, that's who they are!" and went on their way, we would be more accepted. There is something to having a visible identification with a minority, having a skin color or a green hair color. But we don't have green hair, and, it's easy for us to hide, and because society doesn't like us, we hide.*

❤

Phillip 27   *Enough people standing up and saying, "Here I am, this is who I am and I expect to be recognized for who and what I am!" including everyone involved in non-traditional families, step families,* *someone caring for aging parents at home, and all the different combinations. This one, narrow definition of what a family is doesn't apply any more. It was this ideal for so long. Look at all the 50s sitcoms. There have always been lots of families that didn't fit into the role, especially different kinds of minority and ethnic families who were just ignored.*

Steve 35   *Years ago the family unit was much stronger. Families tended to stay put. Over the past three decades, families have become more mobile so you get this fragmentation.*

Rachel 30   *More people being gay and more people being visible doing it. In terms of meaningful legal change, I don't know that that's going to happen in the rural Mid-West unless most states have civil rights protection for lesbian and gay people.*

Jackie 40   *It will take legislation. It will take forcing behavior change. I doubt that attitude change would precede behavior change.*

Lynn 38   *I bundle a lot of things together. I think there would have to be no racism, no sexism, no heterosexism, and that's just a pretty tall order. That same sort of thinking underlies all of those biases.*

Adria-Ann 43   *A lot of change comes when it's forced on people; when they have to deal with it; when they find out their next door neighbors are gay and are Domestic Partners; when they find out their son or daughter is gay.*

Larry 45   *For lesbians and gay men to come out wherever and whenever we can, because we're still largely invisible. Throughout the country, in our workplace, to our families, to our neighbors, we're invisible. They're going to work with us, they're going to like the work that we do, they're going to like the fact that we're good and loving family members, that we're good friends, that we're good neighbors, and that we're part of our community. Not just coming out as individuals, but as couples and families.*

Steve 30   *More non-traditional families being out there for people to see. Most people don't realize how many different kinds of families there are.*

Stephanie 48   *It's already happening.*

More states have anti-discrimination laws being enacted. I work in a youth shelter for homeless kids. One reason gay kids come to San Francisco is that they see it as a mecca. In talking to the parents of these kids, they're a lot more aware and open than I would suspect. At least they're willing to talk about it. That's certainly something different than was available to me as a teenager.

Jeanette 37 *AIDS has a lot to do with it. Most people in middle America think of gay men. People who have come here to San Francisco, are the people that are attached to people there. We see many parents of men who are dying in San Francisco who are from Wichita or someplace and there's no question that it changes their sensitivity, and when their friends know, it changes theirs.*

———————❤———————

Kevin 37 *It will be a legal issue. It will become easier to allow gay men and lesbians to marry.*

Dan 37 *More gays and non-traditional families need to come out. It would be wonderful if the Catholic Archbishop or some big public figure were to come out and say, "We've really re-thought this, and it's really a form of discrimination and we'd like to change it."*

Kevin *It's almost like a civil rights movement, you force integration and later you deal with other issues.*

———————❤———————

Steve 37 *What's going to change America's attitude about non-traditional relationships is television. I think that will begin to happen as soon as gay people are put on TV as people that are not very different from their heterosexual counterparts, for instance, in sitcoms.*

Chuck 38 *Heterosexuals are also adopting more and more alternative arrangements for their relationships. There is more of a material advantage for themselves to understand and legitimize alternative relationships, and that's going to necessarily include gay and lesbian relationships. More of the population will be becoming non-traditional families, so they won't be downing non-traditional families.*

Steve *Non-traditional does not include homophobia going away.*

Chuck *The way it's going to slip through is the way the laws are going to be written about legitimizing relationships for financial arrangements. I think there's a very interesting dynamic in the argument that Marvin Harris, an anthropologist, made. He noted that in the latter half of the twentieth century, as the cost of raising a child to the age of eighteen goes way beyond $100,000 in some cases, and the real material benefits to the family, not the emotional, drop to basically zero because you don't*

depend on your children to work on the farm or whatever, that there is
less and less material pressure to continue being wedded to the traditional
family structure.   The thing about morals and people's opinions is that they
stem out of material conditions.   Once the material conditions change, the
conceptualizing is going to follow behind.

   Steve   *Traditional marriage is set up for children and to protect children*
and property inheritance.   As soon as that no longer becomes applicable,
that is also going to cause a change and lead to Domestic Partners.

---❤---

   Sandy 35   *It begins at home, everybody's home.*
   Annette 32   *It will take a lot of education.   My mom, thank God, is at*
least open to some of that.   I have a Masters in Theology, so I'm able to
talk to her about the church.   We're able to take a look at some of the
Bible stuff that she's aware of.   I'm able to offer some other resources to
her.   She's open to hearing that, though she may not change her opinion.

---❤---

   Otto 60   *The change is obvious over our lifetime.   When we started out,*
we were pretty much in the closet and had to be.   At the time we're
retiring, we could have been out very easily.   This is taken in the context
of San Francisco where it's a more accepting community.   You couldn't
probably do that in Kansas, but we're not in Kansas anymore, Toto.

   I think attitudes will change.   It's happening faster than we realize.   It's
happening in my lifetime and it took hundreds and hundreds of years to
get to that point and it seems like it's racing ahead now.   I would expect
that in a few more years Domestic Partnership laws will be common place
among communities and states.   The private sector moves when the public
sector has already taken the lead.

   Dick 60   *I would compare it to a couple of other civil rights things like*
the black civil rights movements which has transpired during my lifetime.
I can remember when the deep south said, "No, never!"   Well, never is
here, it's all changed.   There are still a lot of bigots out there, but the laws
have been changed to a great extent.   I see the same thing happening with
the gay movement.   Things start in California and they have a tendency to
spread.   The next place is New York, then Chicago and pretty soon it's all
over the country.   We will get civil rights in California.   It's only a matter
of time.   It's a continuing education process.   If it takes a few riots here
and there to make people aware that there's an issue that they have to
address, then I guess that's what has to happen.

   If you're going to give some people certain benefits under the law
because they have gone down to City Hall and registered as a married

couple, then you have to give us the same benefits. It's only a matter of time before that becomes a popular or common understanding.

———————————❤———————————

Darien 47   *The next generation. The two people in our respective families that had the most difficulty about it, in each case, was our mothers. It was the conditioning under which they grew up. They weren't raised to believe in the acceptance of any other family environment. My nieces and nephews are in their twenties. Their kids are much more comfortable with it, at ease about it, and knew about it before their parents even told them about it. Their kids are the ones that are saying to them, "Ease up, she's still Aunt Darien, we still love her, she's fine, she's happy, Katherine's great, David's terrific. Ease up Mom, ease up Dad." They're the ones that will be more accepting. They will change the law and what they can't change, their children will.*

Katherine 40   *I think this book is a good starting point where readers can see regular American people who love each other, who have the courage of their convictions, pay taxes, raise children, stand up and make a public affirmation of a commitment to each other.   Maybe they haven't seen that before. Here's an opportunity to see, to come into our homes and hear what our lives are like.*

———————————❤———————————

Ben 32   *This is a civil rights issue. Nothing's going to happen until the gay community gets angry and does more things in civil disobedience to go out and claim what's rightfully theirs. I don't think it's going to happen over night or that it's going to be this loving acceptance thing. There's going to have to be some sort of conflict that occurs, literally demonstrations.*

The Gay March on Washington [1987] was the largest civil rights march in this century, larger than the Black Civil Rights marches in the 60s and you didn't hear word one about it on the news. When twelve people threw a police barricade through a plate glass window protesting AB101, it made five minutes of national news on every network.

It parallels the Black Civil Rights. You saw a lot of peaceful marches with Martin Luther King that didn't mean a thing. But when blacks rioted in the streets, that's when you saw more affirmative action and people taking that culture and that society as a serious block of people to contend with, both as voting public and in their daily interactions. Gays have a right to get angry and express that anger, and if that means civil disobediences and marches, so be it.

———————————❤———————————

Chris 33   *Just as our grandmothers laid the groundwork for us as women to have a lot of the rights that we have, this next generation, because of the strides that we're making, will have more. It will take legal battles.*

Lee 33   *People finding out that we aren't the horrible stereotypes that everyone's always known. I think people being out is important. That also has to be balanced with your safety, be that economic or physical safety. The opposition thinks, "I don't know any of them. They are these horrible people. We need to protect our children from being near those people."*

They'll change by finding out that this neighbor of theirs is gay. They go to work, they're not insane people, and they're not doing wild sex parties, not that wild sex parties are bad. They seem to have the stereotype of all of the worst characteristics and think that every homosexual must be that way.

------❤------

Coni 39   *Be careful about underestimating the avalanche of opposition that will happen as laws proving our legal rights come more and more into the public forum.*

Jane 49   *As more of us love who we are and celebrate that, as more people come out and this goes into families, the more society will change.*

Coni   *What will change it truly, is one-on-one; me sitting down and talking with my parents, or my brother, or people at work, or someone who feels that they have never met a lesbian or gay person.*

Jane   *We're creating families and moving away from traditional families.*

Coni   *We'll move away from the myth that most of America lives in a traditional family. That's a fantasy.*

Jane   *Change is when power domination moves out of white male power into a mutuality, when we see each other as international citizens of the world, when we recognize that we have great diversity in the world and we honor diversity, whether it be orientation or color or whatever.*

Coni   *When people start making decisions for themselves rather than relying on an outside source telling them this is what they should think or this is what they should do in a situation.*

------❤------

Susan 33   *Things will change if the people that are really afraid of gays realize that their family is gay or one of their friends is gay. They have to be personally associated with somebody to really understand that kind of life-style. If it hits you at home, it really changes things. I think it's* *progressing. It's getting better, but it's slow going. It may never change. People may never really truly accept it.*

Marty 32 *I've found that as I become more comfortable in my own choice of my life-style, that my friends that are straight or my parents or my family will be more comfortable with that. Maybe that's something that has to happen. As each person who is a lesbian or gay becomes more comfortable with themselves and in their own relationship, then maybe their friends will understand a little better and be a little more accepting.*

Susan *It will take lots of work.*

Marty *Being on the more liberal end of the country, it seems like it's going to be a long time before this country recognizes us as people.*

Tell me about living in San Francisco.

Brent 38 *I think the City of San Francisco is to be commended as a city. It is obviously the most caring city for gay people to live in.*

❤

Dan 40 *It costs like a luxury. We take a lot for granted here as a gay couple. We can go, not only within our own neighborhood, but pretty much anywhere in the city, hold hands and show affection for each other and people don't seem to pay that much attention.*

❤

Jane 29 *The acceptance is almost deceptively comfy. You go away and you're in another land and you forget the struggle that your friends in Boise, Idaho are having.*

We've lost a lot of sense of community here. In Boston, the gay and lesbian community is much tighter because they have more to fight. There's fear, so they've really bonded together. There's places to congregate other than bars named "Wet." I miss it, but I wouldn't give this up for the world. I feel comfortable here.

❤

Joan 24 *It's dangerous, because you let yourself slip into a frame of mind that thinks, "I don't have to fight for my political rights, because they're all already here, everyone supports me, the Supervisors support me, some of the Supervisors are gay, this is a wonderful place, I'll never leave." Well, you have to leave. You have to leave physically sometime and go on trips. You have to leave mentally and communicate with people in other states. You can't just hide in this city for the rest of your life.*

Louise 28 *I think it's really wonderful to live here and feel like I don't have to be frightened and ashamed of our relationship. Anyone that I talk to in San Francisco is going to have at least heard of lesbians and gays and heard the concept and that someone thinks that might be okay.*

I go home to Virginia and see how the newspaper editorials see gay men. They all practice anal sex all the time and spread AIDS, they're undermining the family and they molest children. Then I come back here and the Supervisors and the Mayoral candidates are falling all over each other to be part of the kick off on the No on K Campaign. While there are things that obviously need to happen here, compared to the rest of the country, it's fantasy land.

I would like to move back to the East Coast, although I want to have children with Joan. We probably are going to need to stay here in order for both of us to be able to have legal guardianship of a child. It's like being trapped here. We wanted to put our names down as a lesbian couple, a couple of women that are in a stable relationship, just to statistically counteract this idea that gay people are promiscuous men. It doesn't occur to a lot of people that homosexuality outside of drag queens exists.

---------------------❤---------------------

Brad 30   *There's no other place in the world like it, I love it.*

Carl 46   *It does have an environment that is more supportive than many.*

Brad   *We go outside of our warm, cozy world here to Idaho Falls, Idaho and walk down the shopping mall hand in hand. The Mormon people didn't look on that as...it wasn't pretty. It's uncomfortable outside of here, maybe that's why I love it so much.*

Carl   *If I'm out of town, I'm much more aware of what's going on around me than I am here. It is quite different. Driving through Washington and all the government buildings, I felt if anything went wrong and I needed help it would be a bit of a problem, more of a problem than it would be if I were at home.*

---------------------❤---------------------

Wally 37   *If you travel outside of San Francisco, you have to immediately go into a closet.*

Richard 28   *We have to take a step backwards. We can't go someplace and hold hands, because you get beat up.*

Wally   *You're in fear of your life. You don't have to go far out of San Francisco, you don't even have to leave San Francisco. It's luxurious here, but go down some Halloween night on Castro Street. Gay people stopped going because there are so many people that are just there to see the weirdos. The straights all come out to see the freaks. Who wants to be perceived as a freak. Not only that, it's not safe. Why do Latinos, who probably don't really understand what they're doing, feel that they can come into the Castro and beat people up with baseball bats? They don't see us coming into their community and doing that kind of thing.*

Richard   *We'll go out to eat in straight restaurants. Generally, when we go out to bars, they're gay bars. It's nice to be in the company of your own kind.*

Wally   *You won't find us going to a restaurant in North Beach very often at all, and definitely never in the Marina.*

---------------------❤---------------------

Ken 45 *Weather aside, I think it's great. It really skews your sense of the temperature of the country as far as doing what you want and acting however you want.*

Jay 41 *Where else would you live? I go back east once a month and I see people in Washington D.C. I went to the gym there one time and heard some guy saying, "There's this guy that sits in the desk next to me at work and I think he's gay." The other guy says, "Well, how long has he worked there." The guy says, "Six months." And I thought to myself, "Six minutes here in San Francisco and you would ask him, are you gay, do you have a lover, are you single?" And I thought, that's sad. The gay bars there are very crowded everyday of the week like it used to be here years ago. They don't ask all that at work like we do here. We're spoiled and we don't realize it until we leave here. Two men can go to the best restaurant in town, and nobody thinks a thing of it here.*

Ken *San Francisco's a fairly young city. Most people came from somewhere else and, in a lot of cases, were getting away from something. It was Baghdad by the Bay, the Barbary Coast. It's kind of exciting and sordid.*

Jay *Everybody must imagine this exotic life that gay people lead here in San Francisco and then when you look at us, it isn't very exotic at all. We have a normal home. We take out the garbage. We have to pay the paper boy. It's just as normal as can be. We bicker and we complain about the cat, but we're happy.*

❤

Anne 38 *We can't live anywhere else, especially not with children.*

Simone 52 *Remember, I'm an "out" teacher. All the kids know I'm lesbian. The parents know. The principal knows. We chaperoned the prom. I am totally free. I'm finally free. I don't have to hide anything. If I even go across the bay, I would have to hide, I would have to be in the closet.*

I was very proud to be a San Franciscan during the earthquake. It was what we think a small town should be like, everyone helping each other and a sense of comraderie. There were no lights in the city and there was no looting.

❤

Steve 35 *If we leave San Francisco, sometimes it's frustrating. If we walk on Stinson Beach, there are a lot of service men there, a lot of families and a very straight feeling, a very sexual homophobic feeling. It doesn't make for a real comfortable stroll.*

Phillip 27 *It wasn't like a nice relaxing walk on the beach, holding hands and walking by the water.*

Steve   *We're a couple, we're in love, and we want to express our affection.*

---❤---

Lynn 38   *This is like a fantasy environment for gay people and lesbians, pockets of the city, of Northern California.*

---❤---

Adria-Ann 43   *It's a privilege being a gay person and living here. There's so many good things about it. There's every opportunity here to be myself, professionally and personally.*

Kris 26   *Traveling outside of San Francisco is discouraging for me because our vacations are very precious. We work hard all year and we get a week or two weeks at a time and we need that time for being romantic, being together, and being relaxed. It's really difficult to be a visible couple outside of San Francisco. I was in tears the first night in Puerto Vallarta because it felt so heterosexual and limiting. It's this really beautiful tropical place and everybody's in love and looking and feeling great. We felt very much like we needed to hide.*

I feel like I don't get singled out as a target here the way that I would if I went home to Bakersfield. All of a sudden, I feel very large and very masculine. There are things about my identity that come up that just don't dawn on me everyday here. All of a sudden, I feel like a Martian when I'm there.

---❤---

Larry 45   *It's frightening, it's oppressive to be somewhere else feeling the way we do about each other and being frightened of holding hands or kissing each other or doing anything to indicate our relationship in public. Sometimes, it makes me not even want to go anywhere.*

I love living in San Francisco even though it's also oppressive here for gay people sometimes because there is so much anti-gay violence even in our own neighborhood. You forget how hard it is for other people around the country sometimes.

Wood 45   *It seems so perverted not to be able to express our love, their hatred not allowing us and our fear that they will bash us, because they do attack gay people physically in a lot of places in the country.*

I don't take it for granted. Even going to a movie in the suburbs, we're up tight and it's hard to be affectionate.

Larry   *This luxury sometimes isolates you. The Castro is a ghetto. It's been created for us as a safe place to be.*

---❤---

Steve 30   *We bitch and moan because we can't afford a house here and then we start looking around. I don't think there's any other place to live.*

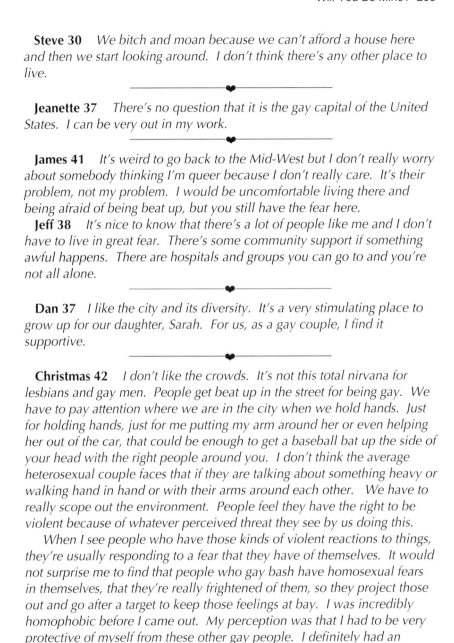

Jeanette 37   *There's no question that it is the gay capital of the United States. I can be very out in my work.*

James 41   *It's weird to go back to the Mid-West but I don't really worry about somebody thinking I'm queer because I don't really care. It's their problem, not my problem. I would be uncomfortable living there and being afraid of being beat up, but you still have the fear here.*

Jeff 38   *It's nice to know that there's a lot of people like me and I don't have to live in great fear. There's some community support if something awful happens. There are hospitals and groups you can go to and you're not all alone.*

Dan 37   *I like the city and its diversity. It's a very stimulating place to grow up for our daughter, Sarah. For us, as a gay couple, I find it supportive.*

Christmas 42   *I don't like the crowds. It's not this total nirvana for lesbians and gay men. People get beat up in the street for being gay. We have to pay attention where we are in the city when we hold hands. Just for holding hands, just for me putting my arm around her or even helping her out of the car, that could be enough to get a baseball bat up the side of your head with the right people around you. I don't think the average heterosexual couple faces that if they are talking about something heavy or walking hand in hand or with their arms around each other. We have to really scope out the environment. People feel they have the right to be violent because of whatever perceived threat they see by us doing this.*

When I see people who have those kinds of violent reactions to things, they're usually responding to a fear that they have of themselves. It would not surprise me to find that people who gay bash have homosexual fears in themselves, that they're really frightened of them, so they project those out and go after a target to keep those feelings at bay. I was incredibly homophobic before I came out. My perception was that I had to be very protective of myself from these other gay people. I definitely had an aversion to and fear of gay men or lesbians. It was very threatening to me.

Darien 47   *I wouldn't live anywhere else. We don't live in what people* *would consider a gay neighborhood and yet we're very open and we're very well accepted.*

Katherine 40   *We're accepting of ourselves. If there were any doubt about that, it would cause anxiety and hesitation on their part.*

Darien   *We're good neighbors. They have a lot of respect for us in how we care for the neighborhood.*

———————❤———————

Marty 32   *I think as far as the rest of the country goes, we're really fortunate. We work in civil service jobs. I know very few people who could be really as open about their sexuality as we are. All of our superiors know it and are very supportive of it.*

Tell me about coming out.

Wade 34   *Maybe in some sense, our coming out process, coming to grips with who we are, is what our parents had to go through. I think in some ways that society now is going to have to go through that. We're at the point now that they recognize, yes, gayness does exist. There was a point when that was not clear. Now people are sort of batting their heads against...it does exist...what does that mean?...do I like it?...do I not like it?...do I want to support it?...do I not want to support it? This country is coming out.*

Q   Tell me about the coming out process.

Wade   *The first thing is to recognize that you are gay, or in the case of our parents, to recognize that someone else is gay and that it is a reality. The second thing is to think about what that means in terms of all of your internal thinking. Your values have certain input into what it means to be gay. You have to wrestle with that and come to a conclusion about how being gay fits into your values. That may mean that you have to change some of your values, what is important and what is not important, and re-think them rather than be saying, "Well, someone told me that this was right or that was wrong." You have to say, "Okay, I'm told that being gay is wrong, but I'm gay and I don't see anything I'm doing wrong, so what does that mean? I'll have to think about this." It's a real process where you have to stop and re-evaluate all of those tenets.*

Then, I think there's a stage where you feel good about yourself one day and feel bad about yourself the next. Then there comes a point when you say, "I'm gay and everything about being gay is great." You finish coming out when you finally say, "That's a piece of my life, but it's only a piece of my life. It doesn't have to consume me, I don't have to yell about it. I have my work life, I have my career, I have my house, and I happen to be gay...okay, fine." It's when you get there, I think, that things are done.

Right now, what we're dealing with in society is probably the thinking part. We've been told as a society that being gay is wrong. Now, we're recognizing that gayness exists around all over the place. Now, we have to start thinking about, "Well, they told us it was wrong, but what is wrong about it and what do I think personally as an individual about it?"

❤

Wood 45   *It was mostly sexual. Even at seven, I knew I was attracted to other boys. At the time, I didn't think very much about it. I guess I knew that I shouldn't talk about it and that my parents wouldn't like it, so*

I kept it a secret. It was sex, and even little children know that sex is something that is never talked about. You never saw your parents do it; you never heard them talk about it. It didn't start feeling dirty until I got a little bit older and developed cognitive and logical skills and then I could say, "Oh yes, they're talking about queers and those are boys that have sex with other boys and that's what I did, so I must be queer, so I must be dirty."

I went through this whole thing of feeling bad about those feelings and then saying, "No, I can't be queer, I have to deny this." I went through this whole thing of trying to be straight and hating myself more and more. Then, there's finally the breakthrough when you get older. The sexuality was so strong there was just no denying it. At that point, I said, "This is just who I am." That was coming out to me. After I accepted this for myself, I sought out other people, other media, books, to teach myself what it meant. The gay movement helped a lot. I found community.

Larry 45   *The coming out process for society had a big jolt in terms of the sexual revolution and feminism that happened in the 60s and the 70s. It sped it up. With the rise of Reaganism and AIDS, we've come back a little bit and people are a little more frightened now. If you really have a strong sense of pride and do not doubt in any way that being gay is wonderful, then I think that sends a message to the people in your life. I said to my family, "This is me. I'm not going to be quiet about being gay, unless you're going to be quiet about being straight."*

For me, I never thought it was bad. I always thought that it was this wonderful secret and this wonderful adventure. I thought I was part of a secret club of superior people. I was in New Mexico where I was always upset by how unsophisticated people were. I had this brutal stepfather and there were rednecks all around me. The gay people I was meeting were by and large more sophisticated and I thought, "These are the kind of people I want to be with and isn't it great that I'm in this club." I knew we had to keep it secret, because you always kept sexuality secret. I didn't resist it, I really liked it. The main pain it caused me was that I feared for my life if anybody found out.

———————————❤———————————

Ken 32   *The whole coming out process for gay and lesbian folks is really this soul searching of, "Who do I want to be and do I want to go against the norm and what's expected of me?" But as a result, we have an opportunity of living the way we really want to live. I don't know if that's so true of other people who fit the norm and go along with the flow. There is no flow for a gay youth growing up.*

———————————❤———————————

Dick 60 *When I was young, coming out was unheard of. Your book can contribute something to let young people know that it's possible to have a long-term, stable gay relationship that's quite satisfying. I don't think we have any more or less problems than straight couples.*
Otto 60 *Young people want to come out, where we tried to hide it. It's more accepting now, so they want to come out and be up front with their life. After all, being gay is a big part of your life and if you have to hide that, it really hurts.*

❤

Christmas 42 *As soon as I came out I sent my older brother, his wife, and one of my other brothers, books about loving someone gay, about families of people who are gay and understanding what's going on. They burned the books. This is when they were living in Alabama. They were all feeding off of each other's anxiety about it and my parents' homophobia.*

❤

Todd 27 *When I came out, my mother and my family had to get used to the whole idea. They had to come to terms with me and who I was.*
Ben 32 *I'm estranged from my family because of the gay thing. I decided to cut off relations.*
Todd *Teen suicide is a real problem. Gay teenagers kill themselves, because of the pressures put upon a young person. I know that for myself. When I was younger, I had those same pressures. There were no alternatives to turn to. I didn't know there was a community. I felt odd, like I was the only one.*
Ben *My religious advisor in high school basically poo-pooed it and said, "You're straight. A big guy like you can't possibly be gay." There was no affirmation or model. I think any youth needs some sort of models. How are these kids going to emerge with any self-esteem whatsoever, if they are constantly being told they're the bottom of the barrel? I think a lot of people don't reach their potential and they end up in the bars, doing drugs, or being alcoholics, as a result of the negative image that they're forced into.*

I came out very late in life to my parents because I loved them a lot and I needed their love, but I knew they would reject me. I had a lot of conflict because they brought me up to be an honest individual with a strong ethical system, and yet I was lying to them everyday of my life because I couldn't admit to them that I was gay. When I finally did, they didn't talk to me for a year. That hypocrisy is really widespread.

❤

Susan 33 *I was in my third year of college. I remember all through*

*high school having this strange attraction for my best friend, but you just
didn't dare say anything. Then I met this woman when I was twenty or
twenty-one, I was dating a man and she was dating a man. We became
best friends and it just progressed to the point where we both realized that
something else was going on. I remember feeling incredibly relieved that
it wasn't just me and that I was not alone. I was really, truly happy.
I didn't have to carry around this facade anymore, I could just be who
I was. It was something I had been carrying around for years and just
never realized it.*

Marty 32 *I was in high school singing with a Christian singing group
and I met two lesbians in the group who started talking about being gay.
I had always been attracted to women since I was a little girl. I can
remember having conversations with a friend at seven years old about
loving other people and how come there's all this, "You have to be a man
and a woman and why can't two women love each other?"...having tons
of questions and never getting any answers to them. So, these two
lesbians in the Christian singing group just kind of took my hand and led
me down this path. It was like, yeah, I like this, this is fun.*

*I think the hardest part was when I first told my mom that I was a
lesbian. She was devastated because she thought she'd done something
wrong. She had this amazing guilt. "I didn't raise you properly. Why are
you doing this? Did I not teach you good values?" For a long time, we
didn't speak. We would say hi to each other on the phone, but we
wouldn't have a conversation. We weren't friends.*

*Finally, we sat down and I said to her, "I've chosen to be a lesbian.
That's what I want, that's my life-style, not because you've given me
anything bad. The values that you instilled in me as a kid are there.
I don't treat people badly. I'm not cruel. All the things about loving
someone, that was stuff that you gave me and that's not changed at all.
As a matter of fact, it's probably more developed."*

Susan *Parents want the easiest road for their kids. They instill values in
you and they teach you that way. They want you to go ahead and have a
life where you're going to be happy and have the life that they are used
to...have your husband, have your kids, have security. I think when you
choose an alternate life-style they see that as a difficult road, and it is. It's
not an easy life-style. They are afraid for you and the obstacles that you're
going to run into. They see that if you don't have that security of marriage
and a husband to take care of you, especially if you're a woman, that
you're going to have a really hard time in life.*

Marty *Parents don't see you as being born lesbian or gay with
predetermined lives. They see it as something that went wrong
someplace.*

Is there anything else that you want to say?

Denise 35   *Gael is not my roommate, she's my lover, she's my partner. She's not my girlfriend, which is what people think. I always want to tell people, "No, no, she is my life partner. She is not somebody who just pays the rent with me."*
Gael 30   *Denise has a picture of me on her desk and all the time people say, "Oh, is that your sister?" Now, do we look alike?*
Denise   *Major denial.*

❤

John 35   *If people in middle America already know somebody that is unlike themselves and have set up a relationship, the homophobia doesn't matter, the fear of AIDS goes out the window because you're dealing with a one-on-one. It is not important for us in the gay community to reinforce our love for one another, but it is important for the rest of the country to see that we're just regular citizens.*

❤

Anita 35   *Before we had our Holy Union, we went and registered with the bridal registry at Emporium and picked out a china and silver pattern. I went down under "the bride" and she went down under "the groom" because they didn't have "other."*
A couple of months ago, this letter comes in the mail addressed to me with Lori's last name. I thought she was going to jump out the window from excitement. Finally, recognition!
Lori 28   *The computer, without judging, just did it.*

❤

Bert 45   *For me, being in the closet is one of the biggest disservices that gay people can do to themselves, to society as a whole, and to each other. When I was coming out, there certainly wasn't the acceptance about being gay. Everybody was in the closet, with the exception of drag queens, who were the total opposite extreme of the spectrum. It was not okay to be who you were. Not a lot of people were telling their families. To openly be who I am, acknowledge my love for Gwynn, and that this is a very meaningful relationship for us, is very, very serious. This is just not another boyfriend in a long string of boyfriends, it's something that means a lot to both of us.*
There's part of me that's thinking this is really wonderful what you're doing with this book and there's part of me that's really angry that you have to do it. I'm really tired of the battles. I feel like the salmon swimming upstream all the time, bucking the system, fighting for my

rights, walking through the neighborhood, always looking over my shoulder that I don't get gay bashed, fighting for AIDS, and fighting for health insurance – I get tired of fighting – I get exhausted. All we want to do is live our life just like you want to live your life and have people care about us and share and make some sort of difference on this planet, so that when we do go, somebody knows we were here, that we had some sort of impact here, had friends and were loved – the same kind of stuff that everybody else wants.

_____❤_____

Roderick 57   *Throughout the country, there's a lot of gay men who live in small towns. There's nothing else for them to do, because of pressure from society, they have to get married, they have to have kids. They're living miserable lives and their wives are too.*

William 62   *Once it does come out or they can't accept it anymore, they do one of two things. They tell their wife, "This is the way I am," or they commit suicide. Suicide is very high in the Mid-West among young gays and older people too. They can't face holding this in all their life.*

Roderick   *The sad thing is that these gays are just as prejudiced against other gays.*

William   *They see San Francisco on television and they see the crazy parades and think, "My God, I'm not like that." They don't see other gays that are just like they are. There's no way for them to know each other.*

I think gays make great parents. Children probably get more love from a gay father than they do a straight father.

_____❤_____

Deena 23   *I think the whole idea of your book is really interesting. You're going to show real people who live together and love each other and went through a ceremony, instead of what you see in the news. It's always a drag queen who's out there in her ballgown. I like having someone show people that we're not all radical.*

Gwen 26   *I'm really glad that you're doing this. Educating people is very important because it's just not such a big deal, it really isn't. It's ten or twelve percent of the population. We're not that different from other people. We don't want that much. We just want basic human rights. We want recognition of our relationships. We want to be able to have a recognized ritual for that part of our lives, too. We're not hurting anything by doing that. The part that makes me really sad is that two really wonderful people that found each other and want to live together and support each other and trust each other is being perceived as an ugly bad threat. I don't see what's so threatening about me cooking her dinner and* her getting me a hot water bottle when I have a headache.

Deena   My heterosexual parents did not stay together two months after I was born. It was a mistake. Their heterosexual, traditional family failed. It failed miserably and it's failed three times for my mother. There's no such thing as a traditional family anymore. We're just adding another facet, another type of marriage to what's already out there.

❤

Joel 47   We chose our anniversary as the night that we first met. So we were going to put a party together to recoup some of the expenses that we've had going to heterosexual weddings and giving presents away. We desperately need a new toaster. We have this one friend of ours that has been married twice and he's gotten two presents out of us and we have yet to get a present from him.

You are a product of your parents. Tony makes a lot of fun of my parents. They bicker constantly. At one point, he screamed at me that he did not marry my mother, and I said, "Oh yes you did." My thought was that we are not unlike my parents. We play cards with our friends, we go out, and we drink and we party with our friends. I have the same feelings about our extended family as I did about my parents' extended family when I was a kid. Most of our friends are couples like our parents' friends were.

Tony 39   This book will enlighten people so they will recognize that we exist and we're normal, that we're family, that we have everything that every other family has...to de-mystify us. There's this panic and paranoia about gay people that is so unwarranted.

❤

Hugh 46   We had gone down to AAA (American Automobile Association) a year ago to renew a membership. There was an option of being able to be considered as a family. You could get a better deal; it's cheaper and both of us would be covered. We were given a flat out, "No, that's not available to you," by this very straight man that was there. Side-by-side to him was a woman who was very interested in the proceedings. You could see by her facial expressions that she was attuned to what we were saying. He said, "Oh, just write the President.," or something. He was quite cold and really didn't want to deal with these two fags who were bothering him.

We went down there one year later, just after Domestic Partnership, armed with our certificate and ready for a fight. We wanted to renew our membership and said we'd like to do it as a family. They said, "Oh yes, we can do that. We just got a directive saying that's now all right." We *were flabbergasted and really pleased. It was a reminder that there is a little bit of progress being made. I am also a City Employee, and as a result, David is able to have some health insurance which he hasn't had in many years.*

Back in the Mid-60s, I was first looking for information about being gay. The most positive thing I came across, which is pretty pathetic, was the Kinsey Report. Just to recognize that I was not alone, that there were other people out there, a number of other people in fact, was comforting. I had no hope or faith that I'd ever find them, but at least I knew they were there.

The rainbow flag represents the gay movement. The rainbow is a variety of colors and that's what makes a beautiful rainbow. We're all one shade or another and we make this total rainbow. The drag queens are one lavender piece of this rainbow. They're not the whole rainbow. To cut off any part of the rainbow, you don't have a rainbow.

David 40   *When I was young and I thought I was alone, and even after I found out there were other queers around, I grew up without any role models. I didn't know any men who had stable relationships with other men. There were no gay men who I knew that I could look up to. All I had were the vague images of fems and drag queens. I didn't have any real positive images. Young people now have more.*

Kit 39   *I keep thinking about a chant that is maybe from ACT UP or QUEER NATION. "We're here, we're queer...get used to it." I think there's some truth to that. We're not going to go away, and pretending that gay and lesbian people are not around is not going to make us go away. Coming out is a spiritual transition point. It's re-accepting, re-defining, and re-aligning one's identity. For our whole society to go through coming out is a hugely transforming thing. If we could see that happen it would be beautiful. We need a large spiritual transformation in this society.*

Carl 46   *I would have to quote one of the women that I saw on Valentine's Day at City Hall who said about her partner, "We are in love, we've always been in love, and that's what this is all about today, people loving each other and sharing their lives." I think, if we can get back to some of the basics that evolved around those thoughts, then the rest of it is immaterial.*

I think educated people will make an educated decision about it.

Wally 37 *My view of straight women is that they've been taught that the ultimate thing in their life is to get a man before they're thirty. I see so many women that are going through this crisis as they get into their late twenties and they don't have a date and they're not going out. Unfortunately, there are a lot of women getting into marriages that aren't right for them just because they have to fulfill this fairy tale dream that they have been taught since they were a child. Women are the ones who want to get married. The straight men that I know are not the ones to really propose. I think it's the women who set it up. I don't understand why women feel that they need to have the validation of a marriage to have their life become a success.*

I was taught too, as a kid, that Victorian idea of growing up and getting married. Well, I'm gay, so I grew up looking for years for the right guy to get involved in a relationship with. I wanted a relationship really bad. I went from one to another until all of a sudden something changed. I stopped looking for Mr. Perfect and decided that it's really not the search for the perfect person, it's the search for the person that you can communicate with and is willing to try to grow with you and try to work at things and try to build something with.

❤

Ken 45 *There are so many people that never hear about these issues. This book will help the people who haven't really thought about it.*

Jay 41 *...or the ones who think they might know somebody that's gay. They'll see pictures of people in the book and say, "These people look normal to me."*

Ken *It will give young people an idea about how their lives can go and what's available to them.*

❤

Anne 38 *Those of us that have made it through the process of coming out and coming to understand and accept who we are, those of us who have faced and dealt with the rejection of family and friends, those of us who have lost jobs for being gay or lesbian or have been kicked out of the service, those of us who have dealt with electric shock therapy, are stronger. We are secure in who we are. We know what's important to us and what's important about life and we go after it. The majority of us even laugh about it.*

Simone 52 *A lot of people don't make it though.*

❤

Phillip 27 *We plan to have children one day, possibly through adoption, through a surrogate, or more unlikely through a female friend.*

*We both really like kids. There would be very few places that two gay
fathers could live other than San Francisco.*
Steve 35   *My mother would love another grandchild.*

---❤---

Kris 26   *It's perfectly fine to put into print the kinds of things that
Fundamentalists think and say. I think that's more revealing and more
damaging than just about anything else. I think they hang themselves
every time they come out with some new argument about why nobody
should be different than them.*

---❤---

Larry 45   *What I've been against so much in terms of marriage, is that
couples go off and they're isolated from the rest of the community, and I
would never want that. Wood and I have so much reality and potential in
terms of offering some sort of role model for other people to learn from,
including heterosexual couples, about how to be really, truly open and
loving and liberated and still be part of our community and contribute
because of the strength of our relationship.*

---❤---

Steve 30   *This country is really enriched by how many different people
there are. I'm really happy we have these close minded, narrow people
who get afraid about any kind of change or differences because that
enriches the world, too.*
Ken 32   *Everyone needs to look beyond their hand and experience the
world.*

---❤---

Dan 37   *We're all living on this planet and we only have so many
years. It seems so odd that as a culture we can't talk about how wonderful
it would be if someone actually found someone else that they really and
truly loved and that enriched each others' lives and it made them more
fruitful and loving and kind. We'll talk about..."But, they're not married or
they're two men or two women" as opposed to saying, "Isn't it a
wonderful thing that someone has found someone." If you want to live
alone, how wonderful that is too, but there's something wrong with single
people, too. We can't rejoice in somebody else's happiness. We always
have to question it and be threatened by it or find something demented
about it.*

*It seems very mean spirited, and it's always in the name of something
wonderful and good and loving, like family values. Is that what family
values are about? Domestic Partnership is wonderful and I don't see what
it has to do with anybody else that two people decide to live together and*

happen to be two men or two women or a straight couple that's not married.

———————————◆———————————

Steve 37   *There are very few laws, rituals, or institutions that gay people have to stabilize their relationships. Heterosexuals have, traditionally, the in-laws that take an interest, the parents, and the children. They can get married, there are tax benefits, etc. Gay people just don't have any of that. Gay people, just basically have each other and so it's harder to make it go because your entire relationship is subject to how much you like each other, not all the other things around you to keep it going.*

   When you're gay, you play with the institutions that are around you and parody them a lot of the time. When I came to Chuck's office to pick him up to go to City Hall on Valentine's Day I started joking and said, "Honey, I need more time." He said, "You're coming with me right now!" and just grabbed me like in an old movie.

Chuck 38   *I told him he had to marry me because I was pregnant.*

Steve   *For heterosexual couples, who do use the institution of marriage, it offers an anchor in the real world. Sometimes, that is an anchor around their neck. For gay and lesbian couples, whose relationships are unsanctioned in so many ways, in fact they're purposely derided by people outside, having a ritual will provide sort of an anchor in the real world.*

Chuck   *Because gay relationships have existed outside of this legal framework, they have tended to focus too much on sex. If there's no legal structure you tend to take advantage of things that do validate it somehow. I think for gay people that has largely been sex.*

Steve   *So often, for many gays and lesbians the estimation of whether the relationship is still intact or continues has been linked to whether sexual activity is still going on or is satisfying.   In gay and lesbian couples, just as in heterosexual couples, it's very common for sex to fall out of marriage after a while, but the relationship to continue. One thing that's been different about gay and lesbian couples is, especially for gay men, that all sorts of other sexual arrangements are usually made quite overtly, which doesn't happen nearly as often in heterosexual relationships. It happens, but it's very uncommon for it to be openly discussed and approved of.*

Chuck   *The movement towards Domestic Partnership is paving the way towards some degree of sexual liberation for heterosexuals as well. So many of the marriage laws are based on male oppression of females. Up until fifty years ago, the wife's money became the husband's money. This* *kind of union is setting the way for greater balance of power between men and women in heterosexual relationships.*

Steve *We're as happy as clams.*

Chuck *A friend of ours had the idea, that since Domestic Partners is here and gay men and lesbians are going to be taking advantage of it more, that Cliff's should open a registry. Gay and lesbian couples should register for gifts at Cliff's. It's the hardware store up the street that has everything. It's like an institution on Castro Street.*

AIDS has had a profound effect, especially on gay, male relationships. This is true, regardless of whether both partners are positive or both are negative or it's a mixed status couple. The social dislocation that AIDS has caused in our community is going to exist whether Domestic Partnership happens or not. Possibly, the anchoring might make it a little bit easier for some couples. Psychologically, AIDS is probably one of the biggest issues among gay, male couples in the City.

When one or both of the partners in a relationship is facing a life-threatening situation, their whole concept of the future, of planning, of the long-term dynamics of the relationship, and a whole constellation of issues like that take on a very different meaning. People start making very different kinds of decisions. Sometimes that can bring people together or sometimes that can cause an awful lot of conflict in a relationship. Gay men's ability to think about the future has been very much affected. I've seen people thinking a lot more in immediate terms. Even in the gay community, there's less thinking about the long-term affects of our neighborhood, and stuff like that. People are caught up in what's going on right now.

Steve *You find a lot of HIV positive people who don't care if they have egg yolks, or don't care if they have a lot of fat in their diet, they just don't care. What does it matter?*

Chuck *For some couples, where both are negative, the way it sometimes affects them is, "I'm really afraid that in the future we're going to be here all alone and the rest of our community is going to disappear, because they're going to have died. I'll be here without a community."*

Steve *The gay community takes things in little steps. You just can't think about twenty years from now, or ten years from now, or maybe five years from now. It's too overwhelming. We're coping with this on a day-to-day level. I often think that once there's some kind of vaccine or long-term maintenance for AIDS, so people don't die or don't get sick, we're all going to be put into mental homes for about six months just to see exactly how crazy we really were during all of this, or we'll all be in long-term therapy after it's over.*

Chuck   *I don't see Domestic Partnership increasing monogamy among gay men. There's an important social dynamic that many gay men enjoy about having multiple partners. Many gay men regard sex as a social activity. Lesbians are much more likely to be monogamous. Monogamy doesn't offer stability.*

Steve   *I consider our relationship to be incredibly stable. We have an agreement. We are emotionally monogamous. You may not have an affair with somebody else, you may not go out with somebody else. Don't fuck up Friday night by dragging someone in here when I come home from work and I want to spend my weekend with you. But, if you want to screw around between three and three fifteen on Tuesday afternoon, I really don't care. If he's a nice guy, keep him for dinner, keep him for me. We see the social possibilities of sex. But for our generation that's how you met men. You met them at the baths. You got the basics out of the way first and then, if they were nice people or interesting, it grew.*

Otto 60   *One problem with gay life is that the young people do not have any role models. For myself, even though I could have been a role model, I was very careful not to get involved with young people because it would have been wrong for me to try to lead them into a gay life. They have to find their own way in. This is a misconception among the heterosexuals. They think that we're out there leading people in. That's not the truth. The truth is one out of ten of their children are going to find their way in. I can't be a role model without becoming legally involved in something that I shouldn't be involved in, becoming a criminal. They could say that I was contributing to the delinquency of a minor if I told them our relationship was good. If there's any question, we'd just as soon that they go the other way, because it's a lot easier.*

Currently, the Boy Scouts say, "We won't allow you to be homosexual and be a Boy Scout." I was a Boy Scout, but I didn't tell them I was gay. I didn't know I was gay. I knew I was into men, but I figured that's all right, when I grow up, I won't be, but when I grew up I still was.

Dick 60   *Their policy today is totally hypocritical. They're perfectly willing to have gay Boy Scouts providing they don't tell anybody they're gay. Of course, that's the most damaging possible thing for a person to do to himself, to pretend he's something he isn't. For the Boy Scouts to promote this attitude of staying in the closet is totally hypocritical. They claim that they're helping people grow up and helping people to accept themselves and they're doing exactly the opposite.*

Alice 40   *We're both in recovery and in twelve step programs. We have the same kind of spiritual base. When there are things from the outside that are really negative or affect us, we know to draw upon this spiritual guidance. That's what has really helped me with my individual issues and with people issues. Live and let live.*

Christmas 42   *When we first worked on this proposition it was right when the earthquake happened. We spent a couple of weeks raising money and doing things to help with earthquake relief. We spent a lot of the money that the campaign workers raised for the campaign on helping people from the earthquake.*

Alice   *We wanted to give it to the Salvation Army and they didn't want to take it because it was from gay people. It was over twenty thousand dollars. They finally ended up taking it.*

---❤---

Sandy 32   *I collect pins. When I went down with Annette for Domestic Partnership, I was surprised that nobody had made any. The next day, I drew a pin design with Annette's help. I had a hundred pins made and I've been selling them to all of my friends. There's another pin that it looks like that's from the March on Washington in 1987. It's a design from that pin. The gold rings are our wedding rings that we exchanged. It has a lavender triangle. Lavender is a lesbian color.*

Hitler sewed a pink triangle on the back of homosexuals' jackets before he took them to the gas chambers. Jewish people had stars on the back of their coats and now Jewish people use the star. There were other symbols for other groups like handicapped people.

Instead of using pink, which was used during World War II by Hitler to set aside homosexuals, I wanted to use lavender. During the early 50s and the 60s, homosexuals who wanted other people to know that they were homosexual would just wear a little pink triangle. It became a symbol of empowerment instead of a symbol of destruction. A pink or lavender triangle has come to be a symbol for the women's community.

---❤---

Todd 27   *The far right's logic is not to allow gays any rights at all because that would corrupt society. We grew up in a society that had tried all along to make us straight. We were born to straight parents. It's not like children are all that malleable, or we would have molded long ago to meet society's expectations. We certainly wouldn't have any more ability to mold children into a gay format any more than we were able to be molded. We had nineteen or twenty years under our parents' guidance to be able to become straight and that never happened.*

Ben 32   *I know a half a dozen gay parents and not one of them has a gay kid.*

---❤---

Coni 39   *It's been so hurtful being around conservatives calling us names and telling lies and scaring the public with things that aren't true and are libelous. I'm not saying anything about anybody else's life. I'm not saying to the conservatives, "Because you're intolerant to differences I think you're a sinful person so you don't have a right to have civil rights." I'm saying, "This is who I am. You don't know who I am because you're not lesbian or gay. You haven't had that experience and yet you're trying to pass judgement on somebody else. You don't have a right to do that. You don't have any right to a forum."*

I didn't always feel this way, but being lesbian has been a wonderful gift to me. It has given me a perspective on life and different eyes to view the world. That has enabled me in some small way to understand, since I'm white, what other people in the world go through that I might never have understood in the least. I'm able to relate to many people's struggles and how injustice has hurt so many people. That's why the passion is so great to help build a world around mutuality, where everyone is respected and there aren't power plays for some people to possess others.

---❤---

Marty   *You should feel good enough about yourself, about who you are and your own choices, and live life to its fullest, because it's very short. It can be taken away at any time. If you love someone, love that person fully and make that commitment if that's what you want to do. My time on the Cypress structure during the 1989 Earthquake impressed that on me. I was a paramedic there for twenty hours, underneath, pulling people out. It changed my life around. It made me look at a lot of personal issues and how to better them. It taught me not to take too many things for granted.*

---❤---

Tony 39   *On Joni Mitchell's "Blue" album, there's a song entitled "My Old Man" in which she says, "We don't need no piece of paper from the City Hall keeping us tied and true." That really says it all for us. Our certificate is no such piece of paper. It is not our declaration to each other, but instead a declaration to our community, our city, and the world, that we exist. My relationship with Joel has flourished for more than thirteen years without societal blessing, role models, or guide books. We have defined our relationship on our own terms and wouldn't want to change that. Given the opportunity, as we were on February 14th, who wouldn't want to march down the City Hall steps like the thousands of couples before them, and be able to say, "We're here!"*

❤

Kevin 37   *In the course of the world, and all that could happen at any moment, who one loves is such a small and insignificant part of life, in a sense. Why shouldn't we be allowed to love whomever we feel capable of loving? It's huge for the people involved. It becomes the strength one has to continue living. The politics of who one gets into bed with at night pale in comparison to some of the other issues facing all of us on a day to day basis.*

If this is nourishing, if this is life giving, if this is healthy, if this provides happiness; isn't that the test of whether something's worth while, not whether it looks good on paper or whether it fits a category that we have arbitrarily set up as the Ozzie and Harriet family?

THE END

For additional copies of

Will You Be Mine?

Send $19.95 plus 3.50 shipping and handling to:

Crooked
Street
Press

1317 Grant Avenue #522
San Francisco, California 94133